A Fist Full of Flowers in the Big Parade

Poetry by Parker Pickett

Copyright © 2021 Parker Pickett

All rights reserved. No part of this publication may be reproduced, distributed, or transmitted in any form or by any means, including photocopying, recording, or other electronic or mechanical methods, without the prior written permission of the author, except in the case of brief quotations embodied in critical reviews and certain other noncommercial uses permitted by copyright law. For permission requests, contact the publisher at:

www.Holon.co

ISBN#: 978-1-955342-06-3

Published by:
Holon Publishing & Collective Press
A Storytelling Company
www.Holon.co

Contents

Forward	xiii
Solstice	1
A Real Politic	2
Current Slang	3
Attraction	4
Basket-Weave	5
Welcome Home	6
The Smile on the Clown is Getting Stale	7
Written on a Door	8
When Children Know Your Name	9
Cog	10
Giant Stain	11
Songbirds	12
Achenbach	13
Jesus Culture	14
Stank	15
Heights	16
A Drive	17
Sun Hunter	18
Sunday August Indiana Country Drive	19
Fabricated Molecules	20
Fingering the Gods	21
Not for Resale	22
How I Knew You Loved Me	23
Futures Movement	25

Mirror Metaphysical	26
Thud	27
Us Fools With Our Dignity	28
Unpicked	29
Slit	30
Beak	31
Diamonds in a Rough	32
Warm Yawn	33
Eat Yr Greens	34
There is Too Much Ridiculous Banter Shared in a Planet this Small	35
Line in the News	36
Them Cages Were Paid for With Our Tax Dollars!	37
Language of the Poor	38
-eeee-	39
Cornfield Cemetery	40
Coronation	41
Shortie	42
I Don't Trust the Rocks	43
Dumb Vision	44
Knock-Knock-Knocking	45
Coin Shortage	46
We Fuck to Mature	47
Picking at Scabs	48
Vying for Space	49
Still Life With Potted Plants	50
Yeller	52
All Dogs	53
Portrait of a Wound	54
Erotic Nutrition	55
Here's Your Poem About that Sunset	56

From Man to Ape	57
Phallic Laws	58
Yacht Club Hero	59
Detached	60
Pursuit of Distance	61
Song for the Brave	62
DANCE!	63
A Poor Man's Heart in My Chest	65
Astral Range	69
From Here to Denver	70
Rainfallin' Nevada	71
Trinkets	72
If You Can Dream This	73
Tight Knit	74
View from City Lights Bookstore Poetry Room, Left Window	75
I am a False Demon Staring Out into the Elevated Night	76
Pose American	77
Queen of All Creation	78
Where the Sun White Hot	79
Hazy Morning Mud Hill	80
Tide Pools	81
Seaside Grass	82
The Final Surfer	83
One Day We Will All Return	84
When the Seagulls Cry	85
Low Tides	87
Want to Find Solution	88
Final Night	89
Salvation	90
I See Forever	91
Crash	96

Gaining Traction	97
Dough	98
Pick Up	99
Neo-Pagan Love Song	101
Three Days	103
4:28am in Pittsburgh	104
Winter Appalachia	105
Glitz	106
Salt	107
This is a Poem With No Words	108
Fangs Aggressive	110
Monuments (Written in D.C.)	111
Sculpt	115
Post-Partum	116
Portrait in Prime of Youth	117
One Smack for America	118
Med-I-Cal	119
Enough Coffee	120
We Went to War for What?	121
Questioned	122
Ape Dementia	123
Footprints	124
Back Home in Indiana	125
A Paper-Cut Will Feed You	127
The Art of Pouring	128
Sun Made Us Blind	129
Bread and Butter	132
Sleep Capsule	133
Harvest Remnants	134
Tree Above Farm House	135
Womb	136

Old Glory	138
On Midday Roll	139
Where Nothing is Found	140
Post-Digital Poet	143
I Should Have Communicated Better	144
Criss-Crossed Stars	145
Find Mark Return	146
Crystal Orchard	148
An History Resurface	149
Barriers	150
It is Demanded that You Grow	151
Wail	153
Look Momma	154
Masticate	156
Pull My Daisy 1959	157
Here We Indiana	160
Kingdom of Daisies	161
Rome Wasn't Burned in a Day	163
Exposed?	164
Big Brute	166
Cave Paintings	167
Monkey Losing Fucking Mind	168
Observe the Evidence	169
Pouring Out of Hearth	170
Upheaval	172
Pulsate Within Her	173
WHAMO!	174
Mother Fly	175
Mud Tides	176
Great Pets	177
Chatter	178

Do the Math	179
Each Strand I Find Splitting	180
Valuable Resource	181
Elvis Ain't God	182
To Babylon	183
Age Appropriate	186
Giver of Curse	187
Snake Bathe for Fresh Light	189
Molt	190
Wide	191
House Plant on Window Sill	192
Cell Walls	193
You Don't Play?	194
History Compression	196
Hippiez	197
To Another Time	198
Death Knows Death and I Know Death	199
Decade Dance	201
Swallow Americana	202
Two Thatched Cottages	203
Rain Song	204
Sketch Under Railway Bridge Next to Wapahani River	205
Rites	206
Feathers	207
Happy	208
Tag	209
Now Heaven	210
Part of that Big Squeeze	211
All My Friends are Deindustrialized	213
Hard Water	214
Beards	215

Classic Buzzkill	216
Pocket Globe	217
Political Fervor	218
Generational Blue	220
Oh Progress, I Love You	221
To Death Where We Part	223
Perishable Delight	225
Redevelop Communion	226
In Defiance of Death	227
Subtitled Politic	231
Chivalrous	232
Derby	233
In Relation to Belated Pleasure	234
After Detonate	235
Break the Cycle	236
Cheap Politic	237
Humane	238
Vicious	239
Even Cowgirls Get the Blues	241
I Reckon	242
Freed From the Bonds	243
A Return to Birth	245
Oh Brave Ulysses!	247
Is this the End?	249
Going Back to Anderson	251

*To my city of Anderson,
to all free poets on the verge of divine madness,
to anyone who is brave enough to imagine and
believe in a rebirth of wonder.*

Forward

Written by Emily Doty

It is with the utmost delight that I write what is to function as the liminal threshold between the reader and what will be read for this collection of poems by Parker Pickett. Ideally, I would like to preface this work with something akin to a summary of every morning-lit kitchen conversation, every pancake breakfast or untamed drive into some miscellaneous wilderness, or the air in the painting studio as we juggled our two separate arts in an ever-growing dialogue about our Being and subsequent Making. For the sake of time and space, and for the reason that I believe his work contains so much of the light of his being, I'll narrow it down.

I have had the absolute pleasure of making art alongside Parker in the length of our friendship. He wrote. I painted. Relevant to both my practice and my day to day living is a question he posed to me the summer of 2019, upon surveying new work and scrambling to understand our ever-evolving selves: "What growth took place?"

Parker is a champion for the process. Not because it is easy, it certainly isn't. But rather, because his philosophical truths of love and light in the world are enough for him to trudge through anything.

What has always fascinated me about Parker's work is that in any measurement of it's growth it has continued to hold a narrative of abject bravery and love for living. His love and belief in us, all of us, is abounding and inspiring. And it seeps through every bit of his poetry.

My best advice is to lean into these poems - press hard into the vulnerability, the uninhibited, breakneck joy and sorrow in every line. And when the poems beckon that you come along: GO.

> *"The impossible function of poetry is*
> *to fathoms man's destiny*
> *and transcend it."*

—Lawrence Ferlinghetti

———

"I am writing it
because I had an experience that was a poem.
Because I am a romantic
Because my life is unfulfilled and I am looking for
new experiences
Because I open myself up to poetry
Because everyone talks it
when they see how very well
I listen."

—Diane Wakoski

———

> *"Rain and sun, a flower has to have these or it will not grow very well. Especially important is the sun, the wonderful and wise sun. The rain falls on the flower and the sun shines down on the flower. That is a beautiful thing. There is nothing in the world more beautiful than that."*

—Kenneth Patchen

Solstice

Open up your door and step into my sun.
Buried beneath thy skin, incinerate your love.
Long live the victim's word, horizons do divide.
Nothing ever keeps its youth except the color of your eyes.

Pull me asunder, I am lost beneath your gaze,
It's the beatings of my heart that keeps me sane.
Drag my body towards your body, I am in your light.
Oh sweet euphoric sun, drain the color from your eyes.

I will take you to the angels.
I will take you, don't ask why.
I will take you to the angels.
I will take you, but don't you cry.

Don't cry.

A Real Politic

It was a case of self-defeatism,
waking up to the news of capital
and nature bowing to man,
jerking steps briefcases direct orders to drop each individual bomb
with the future a far way off from now, no need to worry.
Repercussions precious desirable
even though truth and evidence do not matter.
Do not stand for the redwhiteandblue!
Frayed texture, heartland bleeding dry
as shining jewels of enormity the coasts
glisten greased well-oiled machinery
pushed out to new lands,
infecting others with unethical disease.
Ideological warfare crusading for greed and ego,
the love of laws.
Waking up to the news of Capitol
waking up to drones swarming
waking up to world on fire fanning the flames
waking up to hung necks, I know them well.
Finished with the fighting, or so we were told,
but there will always be some sort of black liquid gold,
a resource to extract, a position of importance in such archaic system
design, bubbles growing 'bout to burst everywhere!
And American dream façade will evaporate with the oasis mirage,
and I'll settle my love within the ruins
of Babylon.

Current Slang

Rugged individualism enhances spires of satirical monologues
plastered across billboards in every downtown and every highway in
this idea America and project and playground covering East to Center to
West all what you choose to touch with spent time forgiving the
clouds when they cry I hide inside and write out stupid
incomplete messages such as this one here right now the lady in
hat she gives a skewed smile after years of living
for someone else the frustrations and regrets boil into hate
of themselves redirected out onto others and even flowers they
stomp flowers I read aloud wild and reckless unprecise measurements
forgive me father for I have sinned and this is only a grave dug
out for written phrases the current slang is already dead or dying
welcome to the new home under a tree napping secrets along
loneliness fingers caress lips and scars all
is well that ends tomorrow and toothpaste you do your job smiling
new white new black culture attack I sigh with the sights
                        of fresh blood pooling
                        concave roadside drains.
Brash personalities distraught and unkind wake up wake up the
alarm clock wake up sleepy-head up up wake up the window is
open and I can hear them chanting out of shame.

Attraction

        You can ask some
         angels to chime in.
      I don't mind we
       are simple till the end.
      Soft breath forests grow
        forever old.
       Don't remember pieces of
       my heart I've sold.
      Silence keeps me wide
      awake hours into night.
     Bloom caress ignore
     the best not quite.
     Fountains dried she
      says she doesn't know.
    Tender feet they patter
     as I choose to go.
Hang on
hang on
hang on there is a noose involved
              today.
       I missed you for
       forever in this day.
       If I said it twice,
        I'll regret it instantly.
       I'm a man who doesn't
        care to sing,
but I sing,
 oh I
    sing.

Basket-Weave

You ask about dawn every day,
> ask about rising sun and trains hollering in distant echo chambers,
> heading back into childhood memories sitting at edge of wooded
> pond at peace, and those train-hollering songs rumble onward
> through Indiana and beyond Indiana to this greater America,
> into a kid's morning first light leak through window
> rounding the edge of serenity and stillness.

And you ask about it,
> nostalgia flowing down cheeks puffy and virtuous for
> such a beautiful human hope getting to you.

Magnifying the resistant fingertips digging into softbelly flesh
> of deflowered America.

Dug in mistreated belittled now sullen through mighty
> rivers and what small towns scatter about the fold.

Deflowered America,
> eyes heavy and laden with contempt from malnourishment
> of the human spirit bread-basket has had no bread for years now,
> decades evened on the Mississippi mudded banks,
> not asked for at sunrise.

You ask about how can we find a bit of love this day
> in ourselves,
>
> in others,
>
> gestures of a lonesome fool dragging pulp-heart
>> to place in your arms,
>>> a casket,
>> and merriment eclipse this dawn
>>> surrounded by vacancy.

Welcome Home

> Return
> Return
> Return, carry my body.

Do not divide, scars visible.
Do not speak, snag tongue.
Everywhere we run the rumble of deconstruction.
Mattresses along roadsides where they belong.
Factories no longer heartbeat, now rubble piles and grass.
Whole life looking through broken windows of collapsing buildings,
> spectral comfort, and even that familiarity is demolished,
>> now rubble piles and grass.

This we act, this we live.
Move about rubble city, share our love through rubble city.
Our scraps and tatters, all of what we have, we give.

She has an awkward amount of decay in her eyes.
She lives the past over and over diner breakfast.
She haggles for liquid bread and never shares her secrets.

My city,
my city,
my city is my mother,
my mother, my city is my mother.

> Welcome home,
> my child,
> welcome home.

The Smile on the Clown is Getting Stale

Hot in heavy monkey fur in palms,
        creased agony and love affairs.
Swollen feet, shoes they cry worn soles,
        themselves all moan together.
White man come and take the sun if you want,
        you've taken everything as it is.
Past and forgiven futures alibis.
No names, I'll remember you by your eyes
        gifted slanted rain.
Bumblebee's yellow brightens up grayscale,
        interact anointed buzzing wings.
By candlelight the room fills up with lonely breath.
Some magic would be good to clasp in joyful recognition,
        arms spread for you my dear,
        said sex has given love a bad name.
Wind is thundering our walls,
        I fear the wolf is on his way again.
        I lost myself because too scared to live.
        Off-set country roads never come to rend.
America,
        we think we are the end and the begin.

Written on a Door

Us people love
    to run around,
us people love
    to run around.

                  Go some
                  where go
                  some where.

Us people love
    to run around,
us people love
    to run around.

                    Be no
                  where be
                  no where.

When Children Know your Name

Calamities to catastrophes, it is sad
when children know your name.
So much for love it's not in others
but you have it in yourself
               for yourself
               with yourself.
Growing self-value puts the system
on its heels, they are frightened
they are scared it is unity they fear.
With tension in the air they smile wide
cracking teeth, all the rage
            all the rage,
              let them know our rage.

Don't lock your
      doors.
Outside is quite
      nice.
Legislative
      suffocation.
Fight to remain
      free.

Cog

Everyone thinks they
still got it that they are young
but people only say that or think that
because they have no hope or dreams left
and have given up.
So they pretend and convince themselves
that they are young because
that is when
they had a chance for their hopes and dreams
and hadn't given up on healing themselves,
hadn't folded into the social machine;
forever a cog,
grinding and turning but
never being more,
grinding until their teeth fall out
and they die.

Giant Stain

Found him no pulse leaning on dumpster yeah it
seems he loved himself too much.

>Love is contagious,
>love is injected,
>love is……
>   yeahhh……..

Songbirds

Stacks and heaps of
ringing halos all bound and
shackled to songbirds.

We put too much on their wings
and still expect them to fly.

Achenbach

Maybe it was when your father shot your step-mother dead in your
driveway when you were a kid, you learning terrified.
That is what made you tough, grow thick skin and a realization
of human love for others, it gave you the ability to care.

On the wrestling mat you were the first person I looked up to,
both of us kids you a little older and teaching me how to be tough,
how to be compassionate for the sport and for others, how to then
turn around and teach those after me what you taught me.

We had two matches against each other, I lost both. The first one
showed me how much farther I had to go, how much more I needed to
work to gain your respect. And so I did, and in due time we found each
other facing off again and although I did not beat you, we both knew
that I could. And in that regard I gained your respect. I showed you
I am tough now, too.
It has been years since those days of youth, and I got the news.
They found you with a noose in your closet dangling asphyxiated blue.
And now
another hero of mine is dead.

Jesus Culture

Pleasure from plucking angel wings.
Jesus Culture hurts these eyes they sting.
Modern needs under shade of tree.
I don't need my back no more.
Filthy hands hide grizzly scars.
Obstruct any resemblance of perfection.
Once fired it'll hurt I swear.
If only this bullet was clean,
 if only this bullet was clean.
Holy water has been poured before.
Reflection in fringes of verdant leaf.
Even the guitar ain't enough.
Dictionaries won't tell us anything.
I'm happy at least that's what I think.
My should've been sister died before she was.
Gotta love you though even if you weren't.
Day is dead so be it I am living.
Just shut the fuck up everything I've said is stupid.

Stank

Dropping flies.
This desert is thirsting.
No wonder hiding all.
Behind reach, phones are lost,
 calls are dropped,
 just as flies.
Carried beyond toil.
Stench of man covers void.
Her wrath of fraudulent sin.
Powerless vacuum remains eternal.
Insanity consumes resumes is end all be all.
Voices rise succumbing to righteousness.
A fault all their own.
Blame shadowing eyelids and fingernails
 clawing at wind teeth marks.
Brick collapsing society all around.
Stench of man.
Fraudulent sin.
Gassed at bedtime, in dreams are answers.
Remember them below horizonline
 where the sun don't shine,
 where dropping flies,
 where stench of man
 fills her void.

Heights

Flags cease waving take 'em down.
Limited in mind all hope in a stranger's hand,
 opened up spread wide upon theocratic desert mirage.
Tidal stream goes off beyond holy cactus blossoms,
 pink and otherwise.
Follow dizzy path, at last;
                              caressed finality.
Power speaking violence through stares of ancient values
 leading to post-digital tranquility.
Everlasting if you bite the apple.

Looking up I see big plane trailing history in
        grand blue sky.

        Goodbye,
 I wish I was born in your arms.

A Drive

And we got in car and jumped out of this gooky
city and she asked innocent "where are we going" I said
awed "I don't know" and she "what if we find nothing out
there" and I "well at least we went for it, took a chance
to find something, anything in this wild collective exist"

>What a way
> the sun shone
> on her hands out the window
> dancing in the whipping wind
>   and free.

Sun Hunter

Point arrow tighten pull breathe,
 no breathe.
Cannot miss the mark.
Over bumbling hills and
 fields of crop tanned dried harvested,
over bumbling hills and
 bovine woolly instinct tighten ready for the cold,
over bumbling hills and
 sky lifted puff swirl white blued backdrop flocks migrate tighten.
 I aim beyond.
 I follow the beams splitting the clouds,
   reach direct into the heart,
    cannot miss the mark,
    and let go.

Sunday August Indiana Country Drive

By means to an evened plane.
Sacred as the light,
Sunday and the wings have ceased,
   resting windmills in shaded corridor.
Open and unwound,
   grateful and profound,
   lost the self along the way continue flowing down.
No matter what's at stake this heaven atmosphere
   robed in blue must pursue peaceful time of due time.
How many among us have choked upon the bread?
How many loves who drown us only dry to death?
   I am only sick of
   calamities and sick of
   waiting for that slow to dry.
Fall this all to sleep,
     go and
fall this all to sleep.
              What the day has spoken of,
fall this all to sleep.

Fabricated Molecules

She is made of molecules each one
    is buzzing neural energy,
  feel with tip of tongue palate of taste,
  exercise flavor exotic and ripe,
 language explosive, juices squirming excite.
Hands all over ridges fingerprints leaving
    evidence fabricated by
        desire by
        disbelief and in turn,
        searching for truth.
"Don't give me no lies," she demands,
        adamant yet discouraged
          with reciprocated distance,
     and in distance,
        defeat.

Fingering the Gods

  Such power in young lives being
   turned on by sonic energy ricocheting
  pounding drum beattitudinal uplift
   and revive proto-sexual desires,
       the things before the physical,
  whatchu mean whatchu say?

Holy magicians our contemporary youth fingering the gods,
lies told legs spread c'mon baby, I want your chance.
Take and come clean,
      she said,
       come clean as if all this was filthy.
And I'm disgusted at myself as
much as she is and here we are bashing
our bodies working out the kinks in order
to attain invulnerable euphoric being,
        everlasting and complete.
And we know that this fuck and every fuck after
will never get us where each of us want.
      But we go ahead,
       fall for our primal demands,
        spent to wake alone and watch seasons
     turn body into wrinkles and ache and eventual oblivion.

Not for Resale

It's been a long time comin/
                        crowd don't seem to moan.
Loud gushing hiccupping effort to reveal body,
   sexual tense inflect hard teeth flex tongue.
Young divided by river when tree cut light linger
  wood sap globule gold to drizzle sheltered reliance,
     stowing laughter in each stammering surprise.
She could recognize greatness in herself,
   whimpering melodic sweet blown across interstate
   illumined road dust headlights and other starlike entities.
What dream of escape when choke of soul is press, stress,
l o n g – l o n g – l o n g sigh for yonder love her madly as
                    she walks right out the door
                    thinking of a new place
                    with new people who
                    sprinkle delicate voices,
        not knowing anything but a cheerful smile
         masking subliminal fear of another chapter
               writ with failure.

How I Knew You Loved Me

Snowflakes tiny fluxuate.
Crystalline structures roam atmospheric,
    grace this land and chest.
Worried not now,
  we all happen at once slight delay.
Within space of delay growth,
     connection, return to one,
       a fight against self.
Battlecry of metazoan rumbling pondwater.
Hallucinations on impermanence reactionary.
  Touch light filtered redefined in eyes on blushing skin.
   Embrace with extension of sadness it is healthy, all-right.
Carving symbols in moss collected walls under bridge train
     roar river babble discovery.
Dance on rooftop memory reluctant to be and to show.
Felt all things before even death no song but this and how
   reasons replace action discredit truth.
      Forget way lost in space.
        Aberration violent severed.
         It is difficult now to move.
      More delay add to it.
    And there is function of emotion with no response.
Unbroken passion, reassemble power, piston it away arms muscle
tear to grow build stronger, more resilient to pressure, as does
a heart with blood pump sustain. Echoes are becoming hums
of existence, trail of gunshots, failure of youth claiming poverty
in modern epileptic withdrawal, flashing bright and hormonal.
What found in mud is found in us and our bodies transcend disease.
Flexing learned aggression in lips smacking lips, found our devils
in each other. Resemble euphoria under light refract through split
fingers, ears ringing from song. Each step more bountiful than
the last, gaining momentum tongue pummel spirit shakedown

ransacked ideas full of privacy. I was yours or so was believed.
pluck strands of hair from scalp, splayed each word every
syllable and danced upon cantations with righteousness and
influence silly divinity, every act defying death. Wishing while
arms in arms and thinking of such thing as an end, value lineage and
process before become now then the next is blurry and to define?
                         To label and categorize what felt together?
                  So much more to understand in each of us,
                     and that is why there is silence.
                 Purity in momentary complete,
                         and now distance,
                         and maybe a little regret.

Futures Movement

At large your heart size of fist.
 Mind think of woods wind woofing.
Rocky shores have walked.
 Beauties shiver lonesome covers linen.
Poor eyesight gateway to soul locked.
 Passage and body blubbery, barriers.
Refine supplies, contextualize.
 Eat with fingers pour out toxic.
No names only words describe
 intimacy with self less fortune.
World has head hung low,
 sunken with futures movement.
Time is an old friend
 and when before free,
 this now free.
Isolation at tip of nose.
 Illusion from not sleep.
 Careful my hands have been too busy with
  mending damage blood pump,
       squeeze and
       squeeze and
      coagulate to cover up and heal.

Mirror Metaphysical

 Haven't felt you in quite a long extension.
Ample range suffocates.
  Fingers press into soft-bellied flesh.
Shredded exotic fury yet motion to find
   that which lost and escaped.

Strange how this world works,
 how you never left and I wouldn't look at you for a while.

Now I open to speak
and embrace fear of new unknown.

Thud

You absent bloodshot gallivanting out
and through doorways unabashed and
unafraid slow clock fuck time fuck
political upheaval fuck society backhand
fallout on earth on fire on fire
and legacy it don't matter conscious
eternal and planet swirl even
though we are gone.

So important to everything,
 we center of universe.

Us Fools With Our Dignity

Earth can shake.
City walls can collapse.
Cross-legged sit.
Eyes filter pain.
Loss heavy, enduring
　culture death, unsurmountable.
Populace thudding through life.
Sacks of bone and flabby meat
　and empty thoughts and
　shallow love pools dried crust.
Big hard sun blacktop mirage.
Us fools with our dignity,
　bouncing misery and rage for
　the space where echoes haunt bloodlines.
Reproduce, marriage, fighting, eviscerate
　families and suckle on limited escape
　into death.
A tough line to walk
　　　　　to balance on while
　our sullen screams are carried into the next,
　placed atop them as a crown of roses and feathers,
　teaching them to succumb to this spectral pressure
　emanating from our void.

Unpicked

   Corn stalks unpicked
   leaning in winter wind
   shielded by tree-lines
   who would let you die?
   No use just grow to die?

   Funny how lacking emotion
    all pretends to be I
     want attention with empty
   who would let you die?
   No use just grow to die?

Too many people I know and have known.
Seeds dropped, planted same place,
 hope for next harvest and
 hope for next harvest after and

Slit

I want to know if you can hear it.
  Here, in the center, quiet now.
There, it speaks along wind.
  Every streetlight going out, stifle.
 In halls now empty,
   pathways dim, focus on space between.
Invite to sense,
  eclipse fear with acceptance,
        with choice,
        with embrace.
A wound,
      agape,
  slight leak when alone and silent.
A song of hollow dreams
  feeding sacrificial slit,
  no festive enchantment,
  no crescendo of fury colliding spectacle.

A simple severance between hope/
                           /bodies carrying
                               the dead.

Beak

Two birds in downtown Indy street
blunt beaked battle,
squawking feathered chest puffed
over chunk of stale bread.
Hunger lines defined
as car whips cuts between dispute
and birds hover distance
ready to swoop back in
for the kill.

Diamonds in the Rough

    Little stars
   appear over steel
       and brick
       and concrete piled.
Weeds spike thistle protrude from fissures,
I knotted hands chain link perimeter,
    railroad tracks leading back
    to crumbled memories…

Under the stars anything is beautiful.

Warm Yawn

Early morning before break of dawn,
 haze settled backroads and low laying fields,
 sky powdered shade soft fade peach
 as cars on hiways humm engines east or west.
Man wakes from night in hammock easy, peace, jolly.
Birds territorial threatening swoop but no alarm,
 hold too much fear to act.
                      On this point where
                      we pause within distance
                      of an edge, fascination and
                      collective tension melds into a
                      warm yawn of simple lean
                      and look beyond,
                      if you dare.

Eat Yr Greens

Blow bubble gum wrong side of
 rail tracks steaming loco
 motive for ache agnostic plethora
   choices eat
                yr
                    greens
  grow healthy big
muscles vivacious turn
                them
                on
and suffrage is delayed
   with good thoughts
      and steadfast prayer.

There is Too Much Ridiculous Banter Shared in a Planet this Small

One thousand lifetimes summed up in one.
    Be still
    yet continue to feel the microvibrations.
Grounded and rooted in light.
  Escape the afterlife,
      bury treasure in the minds of others,
      let them feel human once more.
  Dance out of rhythm,
nothing has given as much as this cityscape,
                this earth.

    I know I am naïve.
    I know I am stupid.

          Satisfaction
          is rare when
          words are bare.

Line in the News

We find that collapse is difficult to avoid.
Prepare for what? We've been dying and reborn since
before first axiom of energy propelled and poof,
 here we are sing consume until erased
                        and all continues elsewhere.
Blow that bubble too big.
Atmospheric placenta burst.
No eat we reconcile starvation.
Easy to forget when asphyxiated.
Topple over building towers disrupt.
 I kinda felt the need to simplify all desires
 just enough to survive and get by,
  maybe with a smile or two,
                        you know?

Them Cages were Paid for With Our Tax Dollars!

Felt the tug and pull of pathways some hidden yet
continue to rage and act as a conduit for
 mouths to meet other speckled mouths
wanting to criticize themselves as politico body.
Figure bent to lift up garbage and coast on down
                          way on down south.
Hey them cages were paid for with our tax dollars!
Hey you ain't putting no action to reaction tell it to
                      the judge the final the say.
White power blonde curls gossip on Sunday morning,
 church bells pound juice poured into city regurgitate
                    liquid bread for the poor.
Each page we tore to erase what is considered bold truth
 released to defy censorship and spiritual malnutrition.
Each newborn slapped awake in static white hospital and
 'member how polluted those beds are?
Body after relocated body maximized product placement.
Brought down from highest shelf heaven and barcode scan sold.
Whipped as exit through slide glass automated drive off into shackles
and eventually dragged frail wreck chained luxury grave,
      covered in reusable laughter and
           disposable legislation and
         mud tracks misleading and
        power concentrated and
 molested withering masses huddling in fear
only for us to realize too late that our turn
                      is next.

Language of the Poor

Man is alive in the animal ferocious waste of attitude
   swung by body buried under mud rust of home.
Grown or so, time span evolving relations,
        how come I've been here before?
News reels pre-occupied don't feel too bad,
    this is all there is.
Poets singing to each other thoughtful, intimate,
   language of the poor, masses struck with logos,
               with pathos.
Pissing on each leave your scent.
       Claim your piece.
Plastering metaphors with teeth,
   oh holy holy yadda-yah-yah-yah.
This room is temporary you are temporary,
   compromising difference, bending over edge
           of exist and learn all.
To defy, to revive.
Cleanse with undress of manners, lock door, felt good
   and pure ecstatic, whitened sheet of winter snow.
Silent and polite afterthoughts a ghost.
Sincerity when exchange monies and that's the last 3 bucks
        I've got and how much further?
           How much longer?
To give up I cannot take, rip self-harm induced by resist,
         I insist,
        pausing to look around and
        back and relearn.
     Steady hand on open seas.
      Forget regrets, there are none, accept.

And yes, until death.
The lengths we go to remember
   that we are alive.

-eeee-

Laugh when you'd want to
unexpect reversal momentum,
walking hysteria born and bred trouble,
touching self with envy of decay.
                       HA
                       HA

All right => decreased,
  ironed out droning with eterni-
                        -teeeeeeeeeeeeeeeeeeeeeeeeee
                        eeeeeeeeeeeeeeeeeeeeeeeeeee
                        eeeeeeeeeeeeeeeeeeeeeeeeeee
                        eeeeeeeeeee[**us**]eeeeeeeeeeee
                        eeeeeeeeeeeeeeeeeeeeeeeeeee
                        eeeeeeeeeeeeeeeeeeeeeeeeeee
                        eeeeeeeeeeeeeeeeeeeeeeeeeee-

Cornfield Cemetery

  I could not appreciate
  burning fickle singe
  eclipsing body rumble body
     emptied on binge of useless motives,
              reasons not worth dying for.
Gate with wood sign letters missing,
   tombstones weathered moss eaten carvings rounded by
      wind rain sun snow,
   hidden out between lively green stalks corn,
    box of meadow enlightened with death.

Coronation

                    Fresh flowers plucked; earthen grave provides.

    Every
tombstone is
   celebrated
with a petite
violet
   splayed
under decaying sun.

Shortie

Shortie is slumped.
He is dormant.
Other smacks head with water bottle,
                kicks rough foot,
                jeers about dragging
                malfunctioning down alley,
                      don't wanna leave him behind.
    Oh,
     how it goes.

Shortie fucked up twisted blacked out against wall brick alley paved,
  robbed of labor but spent out on spice,
                as we others take our hammers
                      our drills
                          our labor back into the building whilst
                      dust spewing out and rising
                on a l o n g,
                      l o n g day
                          in September.

I Don't Trust the Rocks

    Lingering sentence.
               Knotted tongue to church bells
                pulverized by fear-mongering,
               shaken knees with a cool breeze I mellowed.

Young boy says plainly,
                "I don't trust the rocks"
to father they pedestrians untimely grace.

                      If I buried myself underneath your incomplete
                      individuality and struggle then dig me out
                          and let me walk away.
                      Every single stone upturned,
                      and now
                          I walk
                                  away.

Dumb Vision

   Inward brutal landscapes
   powered intuition and
    a long road coming down
    from the mountains.

Two bodies emerge,
 twirling exotic esoteric together
      climaxing serendipitous,
a rendezvous of blissed out fatalists
      parting both in search
        of meaninglessness
          in order to become (?)

Knock-Knock-Knocking

Maybe if words
could torment as well as resolve.

-| | | | | | | | | | | | | | | |-

Back makes a nest of concrete;
　pillow of debris for head;
　streetlight for liberation.

-| | | | | | | | | | | | | | | |-

It was beautiful handwriting
　from a beautiful hand he
　　　shared what he feared.

He shared what he feared.

-| | | | | | | | | | | | | | | |-

Pulled movie scenes from
window sills. Life is still;
　　　　　Life bends itself.

Better in transition of night to morning sun politico inter-tribal warfare
begging dispersed along faulty modern roadways cut-up directionless
appeasing a dull consciousness ordering up a pack of cigarettes/
　　　　　　　(_)　(_)　(_ _)
　　　　　　/knock-knock-knocking on wood

Coin Shortage

Munching on change
    ain't enough
they (fed reserve)
say
    we runnin' low.

Pocket jangles.
Cup in car clinks when ride rough roads.
Pennies heads up sidewalks Mr. Lincoln ragged begging.

I passive dream state clueless beauty
  shelter coyish melancholic rose red cheeks
  under scruffy curled beard untrimmed organic.
I the last bastion of unaffected goofs
  leaning to and pushing, yeahyeah pushing,
  surrealistic envision soiling ordinariness,
  wariness slapped down it bad develop attrition,
  coiled eyes slithering seductive breasts and spread,
  tugging universal sigh under kaleidoscopic canopy amorphous.
        I don't know what waiting is.
  Spoiled lips chapped now (!) synchronized with moonlight,
  arraigned and spent the last of last life back then way back when.
I suffer the same and celebrate the same.

As wont to do,
  rolling home to you.

We Fuck to Mature

           Churn it out slow,
        slumping gurgling freakie-noisey
      victim of sex longggggggggg seeeeeeeeeeexxxsssssssssssss
       expending all energy in action moan action mounting
if ye be a radical cumming erotic stimulate UMPH
        fine, baby, friction texture tingling we gotta
plump handful we fuck when it is your time to bleed
            we fuck to mature
          we fuck it ain't as simple
               bent over and tongue lick taste lapping up
                      rejuvenate press and
                            OHMYGODOHHHHHHHH…

What about after and we talk pleasantries
of existence and what we used to be and
other people we have touched in this way and
now you stand up erect and I beleaguered in cushioned
nest coital scent all over our messy bodies and
I speak what I mean,
            not too long now we used up
               all that time remembering excitement found
                    while discovering the physical definitions of
                 each other's world.

Picking at Scabs

      I imagine the sun above has a massive heart.
      What else is there to revolve whole life around?

It is enough with 9 dollars left and a severed thread of blood.
Some depressive episodes alone fun gloom
      and something about not speaking unless attacking.

I bury my face in my hands,
meager stupid hands of evolutionary fame.
I sleep to stave off stress and ache.

When we choose to abandon or to cut ties there is the sickening
    sensation of failure in all aspects of living.
I am too good at abandonment, and work to alter behavior.

      Could be the function of politics repeating methods of illusion.

    Dig in and dry out too old now to root, too old to learn new blooms.
      How faded all of these houses look now.
Never quite knew what it is to hold such value in my soft flesh arms
encompassing simple hope and fearless assurance of honest truth,
      broken to bits subsiding and hiding within rubble piles
        collecting on open fields dotted by cultures measured to
          be defined and then,
            erased.

Why is it we
are born into wounds
gaping never able to
be quite healed?

      Oh, you know,
      picking at scabs,
      letting blood ooze
        a little each night.

Vying for Space

        In a sense vying for space.

She said I've been
    too close,
        but to whom?
          to what?

          Condescend,
          I descend,
          boundaries flat
          reset we said.

All again
varicose veins
    extend as far as I can touch.

        Pump one,
        pump two,
        love does rue.

           Point minimal
             for
           spatial
              awareness.

Do we put the pieces
    back together now?

Still Life With Potted Plants

        She has a hankering for
        this essential act
           of reliance on the moon swing
              over our round eyes glittering
           with unreleased tension.

I walked off alone onto blacktop
got in car revved up missing
headlight and taillight both
passenger side but I gotta
get the fuck out and move on,
        baby.

        We ain't worth the way we talk.
        I do not define it tonight
           or resent this melancholic drag
           through flesh and demeanor.

I do not know of victory in the world when I look out upon the
squealing masses running gunshot cops called and scene of death
just down the street humble location does not speak of such
burdens.
        At least not in public.

She rolled out her mat and spoke of how I am refreshing and I
felt the overwhelming sense of her heartache, carried by coital
dependency we forgave each other for our truths, turn the lamp on,
when her plants under window thirst for moonlight,
I do not know why she is still here.

We wake in night and we fuck again in our partial slumber arousal
treating our bodies with affection physical,
I am wrong for this.

A Fist Full of Flowers in the Big Parade

It is the sun and the moon is hidden now,
get dressed and we chat and she is heartbroke on life.
Kiss her on the forehead and I step on through the door,
into my car and leave her standing alone in her house,
wishing for that feeling once more.

Yeller

                    He said he had a sharp mind
                    clothed in wool
                            barking up the wrong tree.
"What the fuck
   are you doing?"
                    He whimpers,
                        takes off woolen curls,
                    and begs forgiveness.
"Too late.
   You've
   made too
many mistakes.
I don't know what else
       I can do."
                    Collar tugged,
                        drag out near the old oak tree.
                                Slight swing of roped tire,
                                  supple brisk wind,
          pump
          and crack.

All Dogs

        Habit performance,
       dogs out in alley
        howling barks chains.
    Stiff sadness in air,
     choking on stale taste,
  aromas drifted out and away.
Lungs bleeding with exertion,
tremoring to push to inhale,
     ribs running up and along chain link
       dreading a world gone by
  where tails wag no more
        and paws caked in blisters
and none of us,
    none of us go to heaven.

Portrait of a Wound

    He had a large head
        and a fistful of needle scars
        and one big rust tooth chagrin.

Found out too soon about endings.

        Motionless,
      static tension,
          huddled up in ball fetal
             discomfort along high walls
            of alley domain.

Nothing that can't be fixed.

Erotic Nutrition

Resist decay inevitable delay she spoke affectionate
 of mountain peaks and pinching them between
 thumb and pointer finger, snapping tip as one
 does with wooden yellow pencil chewed by
 boredom and lack of stimulation.
Brush aside crust into valley between
 cut of tectonic activity a wound in
 mother you can see always even after death
 and body becomes ash.
When halfway there and no wake up,
 solitary blistering dream in solar flare of orange cream
 sunfade skies horizon faultline crippled,
 personal gravity sucking in erotic nutrition
 of the youth below all of us.
Cult of Nature sacrificing self for growth,
 blood dripped and dried on earth upturned,
 ready for seed. Common occurrence if you
 let it sprout and grow.
Swarm of insects raising vibration of air in the nowhere,
 disorienting directions but slight love push and
 trail of before now remembered realized treaded upon.
Calling all birds and roadkill pulled apart by rubber menace,
 pulpit on hereditary function
 selected by your gods
 barking mad with
 unfiltered holy rage.

Here's Your Poem About the Sunset

She wants a poem about that sunset
                    the other day.
When she asked in the car facing west
    sloped view launched into
      Indiana highway small talk romancing an idea
      too scared to lose.
And I pointed to the sky,
and I hope she saw what I saw,
And I've forgotten what it looked what colors
                what I saw.
All I remember is the feeling only a feeling,
      underneath softened psychedelics
glowing in another end of golden hour youth dream,
        sharing wishes with kisses
              and do-not-tells.

From Man to Ape

          I would not know how to chew
      if not for you.
       I would not know what to say
      if not for the beauty in each day.
       I would not know who to be
     if not for poetry set me free.
      I would not know of love
    if not for unjust bashful berating madness atop
ocean pacified cliffs speeding down with swallowed sunlight
fear eclipsing my insubordinate reckless vigor and sending
   my elated conscious back east tingling with elevated
  vibrating lyric song I slobbering foolish wail out
    of furious drooling dumbness
      for you.

The ape
beats chest,
thump thump,
knuckled on over
to reclaim vision
of evolution
guided by luck
safe in your comforting arms.

Phallic Laws

    Chair face big window.
      Brighten and enlist us to your glow.
   Almost settled, but here deteriorate in
     image desired, image perpetuate,
    how about a biblical fire?
No need for phallic laws
 ordained by wagging pecker-headed
   self-worshipping fools.
Return to the promise land, they swear it.

Return to the sweet glazed over eye song instead!
   More important than stupid ideaologogues and
    their quest to maintain momentary control power the like.
     Patterned life modernity,
      crystal fragmented reveal a picture.
     Caught them red-handed,
       all of them deceiving the deceiver.
Rotten bunch of apples spoiling each other,
   decay and empty of sweetness,
    piled and rotten to the core.

No one cares about your dick,
                  your god.

Yacht Club Hero

Mafia nosed donning jewels hereditary
slicked back hair she nestled car door
open beep fuck the key mustard colored
gas spread out with flat face knife on
sandwich bite me screaming flesh cook
me cracking trees cooking worms fresh bark
no bite until saved world you eco-capitalist
consuming tattered plastic wedges yacht club
hero bubbling fizz boiling fibers into broth
sip shine stream atomic release minute color
of rainbow through prism oil slick asphalt
and piles of cigarette butts chewed on by
kids who wanna look and therefore be *KOOL*

Detached

                Are you able to hold on?
                        collected yrself?
  Winged clipped varying sound
 if form to func
      tion (shun)
    dee
       vide
       visive
Leak milk mommy
glands leak mammery mommy milk mommy
      cide (side)
      cry
    dee
       value palp heart vigorous
          palm crease hand
           dangerous building tall glass
        no money no money
Leak milk honey
Please driz honey gilded honey milk please
          violence is the answer
        if physically confront
           honey milk please
        if physical assault
  (i.e. murder)
       use physical presence
          to hold on?
        collected yrself?
Something on body parts reacting independent (separated)
      of thought.

Pursuit of Distance

Dust particles suspended in light,
    waking to sunrise passing through open clouds
    and genetic function.
Ribboned colors split molecular refract,
 on each body skin tingling hair lengthy ends,
quiet dust settle under sight of moot eyes,
    cornea gelatinous convex pursuit of distance bending
and how this heart shines late upon each battered face.
  Teeth carved by acidic and by chew residue food dissolve,
                             moosh hunger.

Silence,
    we have nothing to pretend.

                Dew-frost cover rust of town.
                Slow moving,
                if at all.

Song for the Brave

I want to live!
I yearn to breathe again!
Choked by the needs of youth and finding only lies.
So, where then is the truth?
Hidden by the winds of change?
Innocence decay in the rush to be brave,
what's left to save?

All there is to give, all our light that tends to bend,
sent out to lose our ways and never realize.
So come clean today!
I will not feel you again!
And it is okay to lose
this struggle with fate,
but it is not too late
to believe in love and blue skies
and how the sun will fall just to rise again.
Pushed past the edge of everything we have known,
left all my love back home for you.

DANCE!

                DANCE!
Limbo under horizonline horizontal escape,
flesh feeling small wounds
  and an upright man
   pushing junk onto babies,
             badda-bing
                  badda-boom.
Electric wizards send computer nonchalant message over intrawebbing,
              glued into digital memory,
                  collect data and as long as we have power we
                got you red-handed!
Fingers slipping through the cracks of isolationism,
              hatred toiling shambles
                guilt of being alive when born of death,
                      last luggage packed and now we roll
                      on the train cars to sunny paradise.

              DANCE!
  If you do not believe then whatever,
  children still smoke tobacco
  guns still freeze lives
  (I hear them going off outside my window in the alleyways
      near eastside Indianapolis)
  dogs bark and sniff the air to know who and where and why and
      how,
  trees shake in wind your own head bosky superstitious
 not allowed to think that far or look that far into own
            disease will block out
  so the new year will be glorious.

All my heroes
are dead and buried

with epitaphs chiseled
into the dome
of their exasperated
      skulls.
                        DANCE!
                  for we have no other company!
                  for we have no other momentous occasion!
                  for you and I are alive again
                    and able to talk and love and jubilation
              dogma of each chemical reaction
                blessed by body
                    by mind
                      by gracious everlasting birth
                      fused within the foam
                        of salt sea spray
                      ascend.

A Poor Man's Heart in My Chest

There is no day there is no night with treetops covering
phantasmic jewels of the skies, no timekeeper in head all-good
veins flowing nonchalant, fire fuses with air surround,
I see with oval eyes blinking stupendous perception
has awakened, one sold-out brain plucking love from memories
drowned and suffocated in oceans of phrases divine, neo-fantasies
driving sell-phones to vibrate more in pockets and
purses, I am shoeless digging out artifacts I hid myself
to show I am a feeble man too caught in personal destiny
and strung out lapping on surviving tatters of papers containing
some philosophical bullshit, the nooks and crannies can't hide forever
but all the same neither can I sorry for the deals,
    retaining glory maybe if I even have anything glorious.
So little heart waves back to Indiana, you are childhood,
you are lotus magic, you are willow trees resting over peaceful pond,
you are dirt, dirt cities rusted shut faces pale and coarse all ends
    start with life.
There and now with pastures forgotten I realize my fear of
vacancy strikes with an invisible force esophagus constrict meltdown
    siren BEEP
siren BEEP although I wish I was the kid in the library, he had the heart
the heart to sit wayside corner proclaiming "man down, man down…"
repeatedly, and now that phrase is glued into my skull one or two days ago
some liar, I mean this is life and every moment spent awake is beauty.
    A poor man's heart in my chest, so why smile so often?
Dragging self into fear and silly recklessness and
    brash confrontations of truth,
feeling exceptional and fully ALIVE!
    Personal group thought daze sessions of
unclouded consciousness the cheap earth to walk along oh sincere
drawn out virtue-lesser-man-dysfunction of sweet
    cold-bloodied America, what a hug to need.

Filling stations beacons of violent refuge and in the single room restroom
mirror scars and tattoos, face reflected back and now feel more with
each who left their marks here, sink on rinse face with water,
there are my eyes and your eyes and fruitless tongue hangs limp,
scrutinize dream world epic revitalization swung over on tire swing
we never had nor ever really wanted and hands get hairier every
fresh mirror check, cheek bones teeth bones,
     where is desperate and faithful hug that I need?
Wound-up in pillows and sheets, some vitamin heavy insomniatic princess
dreary hearted cosmic denying she is a face I've never met but still know
too well, all pleasure all pain all aside, get a grip explaining to self
every few seconds a child starves or an addict overdoses or a family
is now separated in gloom or the summer where first experienced
sexual physical connection and now to current state of mind,
     some new age rite of passage I guess, choked on saliva
     and snot and tears.

                                     Isolated,
                                     isolated.
Sung far off immeasurable distance,
a simple rogue lackadaisical yet true as blood,
  simple and intricate as shine of sunflower,
   soft and power as human smile the human condition
                      in the now oh wow.
An oceanic blue wings around overhead and in touch,
                 what is war?
          Again,
                 what is peace?
All beauty aside people constant change and are better for it
        while tumbling world suffers enough.
                 I am a coward,
                   by the way.
               I know not of bravery,
                   just as you know not what your
                       name truly means.
Filtering bragging and fading fast there is wonder again,
now come on out from your love seats and hop on coffee tables
     to yawn oh mighty and declare that ideas must happen!
A perfect way to respond spending night after night coerced from

A Fist Full of Flowers in the Big Parade

self-isolation to charades with good friends only to discover I want
to bathe in her aroma and cradle her and to know not who she is
and if my wish is granted I will not be saved, continuing lonely
emotional mutilation I AM NOT CRAZY!
                              I am human,
reminded of lovely mistakes and growth from them,
                    thin eyesight,
     tell me what is the difference between time.
Bend in awe of setting sun outside wide St. Louis gathering steam engines,
tone of voice in head excruciating expanse of minuscule loneliness
brought on by degenerative human social interaction but the need,
                lunacy lunacy lunacy!
       Forever is never long enough.
Theatre marquee dormant and babies crying breast milk parables,
  such is the music of Autumn Winter Spring Summer rustland home.
Neon signs unreliable, us half-heartbeat consumers attracted,
  buzzing flies our compound eyes reflect pain, hunger,
     what secrets are kept forever from this world.
Now sunbeams shelter whispers between frantic daughters and
  radical lovers twist me, tuck under the loose visionary relaxes,
     gives pleasure in cacophonic release of
    free-will forming and dancing,
            silly dancing is freedom!
                Dancing in stupidity and shock!
                Dancing rainstorm naked vibrant!
Eyelids do not dare close for there is always a chance that life produces
  a split second of radiant beauty, mesmerized under buildings darkening
     streets of resting hilltop bleed gold San Francisco,
        are you new age too?
Towering sight lifting and forgiving on broken concrete,
  bare-bone shock treatment I am no savage,
              I am beat.
Weary in sadistic rush knowing death loves life oh irony wasted on
  minds of bland youth bleary stains of ignorant regret for what has not
yet happened, sad death realized only a moment too late for bitter ashes,
                                                     ashes.
The wind will blow us down exploring next to each other the sky itself
creating reasons when there are none, how simple and easy, deep blued

fingertips tap-tap-tapping on doors hoping you'd answer one day but we get in the car and gallop somewhere old, somewhere reimagined with budding gilded gleams gush to spill on floor.
A daydream through window blinds.

    If you could drop the leash get outta my fucking face
only for me to lean back in and kiss you on the top of your head,
        all the kids are acting strange,
      it's 2am and I am wandering our streets again.
          This time with less of a presence.
          This time with vacancy on my mind.
          This time holding hands with myself.

            Be gentle,
         for we live peaceful
      to someday die and be free.

Astral Range

Mixed media looking back down on Earth.
Calm,   milky swirls,   out here.
Thirst for below,
 sip cup of society no change,
 shaken deliverance of evil.
Bargained unfair with magic.
Astral range expedite,
 eyes folding with bleakness devoted to
                    divots of light,
                flickering on/off on/off.
Swept the dust of a billion or so odd years
   and tossed it out.
            Goodbye,
                    forever.

From Here to Denver

From here to Denver we watch sun fall envisioned,
graceful fogged flatlands form ridges bursting earthen hands,
    these hands begging towards heavens,
      these hands cupping holy-spectred Denver.
  Oh hip and new-youthed Denver raised above these states!
    Gateway to mountain paths,
nestled in the spine of America you pacified glorified
                      loose-lipped Denver,
                            our ways run to you.
Open armed and in pieces,
  you'll collect our beaten bodies returning our spirits to a glo,
sending us off westward where America takes its resurgent stand.

And I am here with you, oh Denver.
 My love is growing tall
     leaning against
poignant mountained hands.

Rainfallin' Nevada

There's a rain in Nevada,
there's a rain in Nevada.
Cooling dust and sun does hide,
fog shrouds lands between mountainsides

Nevada, are you thirsty?
Nevada, fill your sky?
Nevada, give your love
 so my spirit don't die.

A rain in Nevada
oh yes, a rainfallin' Nevada.
Dry bones,
dry love,
come a get your fill.

Trinkets

    Somewhere outside of Barstow
    carnival station trinkets.
   Circled by the fence,
    marijuana shared,
     train come hollering.
     Union Pacific.
     And jokes,
     and the clean California night,
     and we go off again down the forever roadway.

You Can Dream This

And to breathe again.
   (   )
Shimmer city exploding
out of darkened countryside.
   (   )
Peace settles hectic thoughts as
   we all keep rolling,
        growing,
        moving,
only to find out who we are.

Tight Knit

An arch of gold beaten to a bronzed glow.
A cove in tight knit San Fran Chinatown.

   Leaning against left side is
 a woman calming her woeful child who is
       crying in the simplicity of being so young.

To their right an older woman,
 elbow on cart, purple jacket under overcast,
 gray haired bun pulled taut.
  Older woman stares direct at me across this street
 with a face of wizened grace.

Silent crimson paper lanterns strung from them to me.
     Oh, crying in simplicity.

View from City Lights Bookstore
Poetry Room, Left Window

Clothes hung out to dry between the buildingtops,
      hung outside the windows above the
            modern day graffiti

WE ARE ALL BLEEDING

            a seagull is drifting
          over the gutted brick,
        drifting on to taller towers
            in the distance.

I am a False Demon Staring Out into the Elevated Night

I am a false demon staring out into the elevated night.

It is the roaches who do this.

We all live with a cold list of hate for what reasons?

Force-fed dreams of political kings,
money is sugar so sweet do have a seat on
the weary alleyways and dogs stay far away because
they know your smell.

Hell, part of the reason/the wrong—   who knows?

An addict of lies comes up to me as I am in
Jack Kerouac Alley in San Fran and I give him two bucks
so he can get his fix and I see him all walk all happy
that he fooled a dumb kid into giving a junky a couple bucks
but I saw him and his actions from the start.

I can't help but care for the sky and the lives that rot themselves
out and in the hell of this world.

Look up to see a streetlight glowing down and the
                            zig and the
                            zag of the fire escapes…

All these roaches fleeing, fearful of the light.
        We fear the light.

I am a false demon staring out into the elevated night.

Pose American

Barefoot patterings lengthy between
 each smack of padded foot
 tamping tough ritualistic fervor.
How age increases ache bones
 and aggression recedes to escape in limitless
 white of eyes rolling back into skull
 scanning ideas for reason and acceptance
 of what was envisioned beneath rotten veneer.
Fresh frontier layered voice, moonlit song
                 on the river babble slow.
Brick roads revealed and I've never loved
 the feel of asphalt I've only loved the speed
 across blacktop pushing to eclipse sun.
Even so, there I ache in shame and guilt,
  harboring rust freighters along rocks of west coast San Fran bay waters.
A silent denouncement crude unworthy wallow defeat.
Foghorn knock-out gut-punching knock-out sky
    for I am there 6ft and sinking.
Starved gruesome lunatic pining for moonlit song
                on the river babble slow.
Wailing in pose American,
 fumble thumbs wiping away shelter
 settling into static concrete jag as
    others pass on in stoic revolt.

Queen of All Creation

   To be the queen of all creation.
 Whispers revolting sacred ghost.
 Deity pursed lips scowling hard brow.
 Lion's mane flowering roar wriggling frequencies,
 hot air rising and fluctuate harmonic manipulate.
 Scuff brick with flabby skin.
  Insert raw unlivable but somehow survive, baby,
 dig spoon head pull out it wrinkles flatten.
No longer worn by age
 when all was seen in black to gray to white
and liberty was not seen as foul
and not one was equal enough as it was/is/will be.
   How about good naps, erotic him and him playful?
 Wetted kisses under big oak tree
  piercing puddle sky backdrop all sight of this.
The corners not yet defined
  unless you plow your fields with hatred,
  unless you claim ownership to all things but your own.
Disruptive siren muffled calamity.
       Echoooooooooooh shiver round our doors.
Ain't it lovely to believe in the future?
 We stare out of door, city is alive and well
  masquerading as each love we leave behind.
Resolving movement of modernity, brittle backlash.
Tend to doofy cattle herd mesmerized by blatant cowards
  washing in her royalty,
    majestic fury of the sea.

Where the Sun White Hot

    Sun direct above
     open skies ocean glass
    triangle silhouetted sail
    in vantage point light.

Where the sun white hot divides the blue,
    separated by sky too soft,
        passion razor-slit gradient fading tips,
      reflect and burn crested face of blue,
       consume and fill to sear eyes
             and therefore sear heart.
    Each wave collecting white light eternal
and faulty leaning
        dreaming to become disarmed.

Hazy Morning Mud Hill

Hazy morning mud hill
rain down San Diego.
Sheep graze patchy green hillside,
palmed cactus pads lining their enclosure.
Man gaze easily on wool,
flock calm upon hills,
houses peaking and obscured.

Tide Pools

Skip on rocks seaweed carpet shag
 coral coves for soft-shelled creatures.
Out goes the crowshing,
 gulls perched yawning,
 coated twilight falling.
All minds buoyed equanimity,
 calm drift into gradient of gone.

Seaside Grass

Bulge of seaside grass
  combed by salt wind spray
    and I sit on thee,
  cupped by cavernous cliff behind above,
soft plush sun-bleached green,
    rocks a barrier between raging surf
    and out past breakers connect,
                   centered,
                full,
      returned to birth.

The Final Surfer

As the sun sets,
as the tide flows horizon,
as boats anchor and dock,
as great white gives up chase
    sinking into greater dark,
as loves lock lips sync to crowsh mist,
as children run and parents play,
as stars align reveal place and time,
        he rises from ocean board under arm,
        drenched in freedom and dazed from battle,
        and catches one more wave home.

One Day We Will All Return

                       If yo
                         u cu
                        t ou
                        t th
                        e mid
                          dle of whatever
                is bothering then escape
                        eas
                          e
                        out.
She porcupine quills stabbing owwee pricked mine own skin.
    I lost it,
           there was a snap yesterday and click turned off.
      Seduced by
      a rainstorm.
      Flushed by
        swift big floods.
    Oh well,
          rinsed right back out
                    to sea.
I think,
  in the end,
that is where we all belong,
                the sea.

When the Seagulls Cry

           It is the fizz of sea air bashing joyless
        greywash skies unrelenting,
   coastal waves die crowshing exeunt into smooth rock shore.
Lungs open fresh invigorate zealous tinge to voice.
   Collision of youth and of age,
    transitory the sun burns through clouds casting.
Fade warmth into elevated body transcended.
     Sand built up spill under beatings of lifetimes.
         Piled rooted stories keep hold
      of what is sacred between all of us.
 People migratory ocean oblivious cupped feathers of gull gliding
  over boundary dividing land and sea,
    where birth and death meet.
Fresh scent of brine weaving clothes fabric.
 Love coy no more repent qualms with disaster.
      Accepted, come here disaster!
          Come seduce with your fury!
Hands fold monuments built,
 there is a new age of reason constructed from fields sewn with harmony.

I am the sea.
Lost child epiphany.
 Violent compassion
bring safety and I recede
only to return and swallow all bodies.
     Return to birth.

                Refuge from this world,
              distant and alone on brink of
             oblivion, picked up by wind, sails
          taut tug body into new frontier, displace
        atoms vibrate in empty, oh to love you so,
       watch methodical revolve earthen resolve life

without deliberate function constricted by time,
laborious time. You
      are
        LIBERATED!!!!!
Omnipotent beauty creased in palmful of stardust come settle in
eyes on our miniscule existential ferocity, the looks of hope hidden
behind sunglasses roaring freeway blues windows down let me at 'em,
to reconcile defeatism letting go of all fear,
    wind down from courageous extension
     of contained glory simple-hearted being,
        crowshing exeunt into smooth rock shore.

Low Tides

Electric dayglo orange
  engulfed by vibrant fluxuation
of seafoam green rising falling,
             giving taking,
and afterglow settled in silence.

Skip
       and
  a hop.

Want to Find Solution

Thick slime green algae grow hair length on
    boulders sanded sunken swept
by ocean rise and fall,
       the story of life.
City is melancholic.
   All shoulders slumping in wind
     my hair gathering and whipping.
Want to find solution.
   Reflect overhead sun bleach eyes
       and tongue coated skin salt-mist.
 On pointed tip of cliffs lungs align with
 timing of shoreline crowsh,
       curling epiphanies tucking
      into folds of your lips,
reasonless in wishing and grown accustomed
       to defeat.
    Far, far away
   where the children tend to cry a little longer
   and the sky changes colors a little slower
   and the people drift in endless spectre,
 following each decision decided with contempt.

Final Night

  She stood under streetlight haloed above.
Sweet, sincere, fearful, in her eyes as
  nurturing as forgiving earthen fields of
my Indiana.
      She points her beauty to her left,
     a cigarette between
              ruby red lips.
    She reminds me of my Indiana home,
      simple with a radiance of life and
      in her song and heart is power,
                is desire for more,
                   for eternal.

I do not know of anything
    besides this moment.
 And it is lovely,
         this final night.
 And she is pure.

Salvation

It is the push which shapes us.
 Long winded phrases whipped by modern jargon frenzy you
 sick-sick and potential wide America, loud abrupt implosion,
 virulent noises riding divisive, attitudes portrayed face but c'mon,
       quit yr lyin' to yrself.
 Baptized collect tension stepping find shelter decayed leaning too far
  to be safe beatific too young to die yet too old to be young,
   screaming folly of mankind,
                    far away she goes again.

If I can believe in anything,
  then I choose to believe in love.

  Simple, need nothing but redemption dream.
   A salvation in this life,
                  not next or after.
        In this life,
     maybe with you until you leave too,
                    far away she goes again.
        In this life,
   ease reluctant brave chanting delivered henceforth messengers rebellious
    free-will and gracious power of choice.
   Inescapable vision remind every now and then that all is good and true.
  I believe in your raucous smile just as the sun will rise and the waves will
    crash violent along shorelines,
 heartbeat doldrums linking blood wrapped in the golden burn of all things
    christening our return to righteous birth.

I See Forever

    The thought that we can turn off the sun,
        that we have the power to flip the switch
      finger extended and there,
          no light.
    An overturned cinderblock what's that chain-link fence
    surrounding vines and shrubs nothing 'bout nature and
      the curbs are flattened rounded with silhouette of
        barbed wire strung taut from cloud to cloud.
        What is a budding flower anyway?
No finer connection point between reality and sensuality as some nights
I am amongst friends in body but every being that completes me is
in contact with subpar oblivion,
        oblivious to the most minuscule distance
    between feet and floor when we stand up to feel taller and gaze
      lazily into a road with more car headlights dulled yellow hue,
        what future when path is set too straight for laws of nature?
Already stone,
already outline liquid blood,
    c'mon now!
        A bullet shouting in freedom leaving smoky barrel
          as it dives to embrace the heart of a kid,
        just now learning that love is pain.
    And how about it,
    redblue and swarms of neighborhood families step out to view
      one of their own taken in cuffs.
    A little bit later the event subsides but mother sits on
    fold out chair facing spot where her child was arrested.
        She's on front porch face in hands,
          wearing a sweatshirt and sweatpants dyed pink,
            but the color is draining,

                                        hope is fading,
                            from outside nothing seems different.
         And that's the way
         the world works.
         And that's the way
          the world works.
                    Give out of body and then realizing
                after wake-up from night of uninterpreted dream visions.
These woods sound nothing but brush of foot through undergrowth,
                      far off rain showers calling this way.
                    And that's how it is,
standing in an open patch of grasses with rain thicken.
I stare up catching raindrops in my eyes,
   a lovely sight waltzing through trees,
drops pummel atmosphere as they do
 on car window glass one mile at a time when rushing west,
 out yonder beyond my mudded fields and
treelined hills of s l o w – s l o w Indiana.
     See the fall of the west?
   Land and civilization turning inward
    tucking cities and mountains into sleep.
     Roads curled roads frayed such as ancient scrolls
 unwound after many millennia,
                         r o l l e d,
                          r o l l e d,
                          r o l l e d…
  And man has no such thing as mercy!
  And man cares not for those who live short!
  And man claims victory although there is no war
                      except the war with one's self!
The sky is division,
clear and precise fracture line rides along clouds the world over.
   Speak from our own point of view,
           film rolls abandoned,
      snapshots of glorious history unvisited and forgotten.
    Time is a lovely killer covering all with sand grains from sea to sea.
     Spent hours gazing down railroad tracks leading to some other
          town and city.

A Fist Full of Flowers in the Big Parade

        Imaginations have some use.
      Don't give up your heart and love for life.

You pour on my head in
  the afterdark.
Longing for special summer day
  lightning stripes.
Lengthy crystalline fingerprints,
   Mesozoic standing through time (!)
Thaw, freeze, rain
  proportional with molecular connectivity,
    cities soak in as a sponge!
A gift for the war on last winter!
     What laughter dried from misted treetops,
   it's cold out on this first night.
  Oh society engraved in brick buildings,
       keep on rockin' in the free world!
  Lift them from the gutters!
      Those who beat upon themselves, pressing on bruises
     blued from the craze of America!
  Glued eyelids squinted shut and purposeless
         my friend vomited in a puddle middle of sidewalk
        power heaving from chest through mouth to rinse in
       the inhuman rain.
     Zero tolerance out in the elder states ranging from
        questions about why money is where it is
     and events unfolding to step-by-step record
       the end of last millennia,
      into the new frontier,
     the old ways are flawed the new ways untested and my oh my,
  the kids are brave souls growing up with
 no intentions except to live free and love mighty!
  Cultural nightmares are beyond the point
            and the road is drifting on this night the
           streetlight goes black I am an
          astronomer realizing a far off star has given up
        and poof (..!...)

A skyscraper giving scars to blue tinted atmosphere
rhetoric on the street vibrato suitcase encasing open letters
>> but hell,
> who reads anything anymore?
>> Paper stacks on basement desks every home in America only thinks about the future or nothing at all.
> Close-minded loudmouthed hey robotics got a way into our skulls.
> Love the humming,
> fuses burning and the digital clock beeps in the morning,
>> sunrise/sunset,
>> what is different?

You know I walk outside and think to myself, I see how the world is
and I see how I move how I view the world and how each day relates
to each night and overall nothing has changed from when I was a kid.
I look to a flower and enjoy the flower, I look to the passing traffic
and people nothing different. Buildings gone and now empty lots but
the land has always been there not one thing has changed, I might
be older but damn the days are only shorter than before and trees
fall circle out and in and back and airplanes ride above with
a curiosity sparked inside,

> and I sit out in downtowns the people they are moving.
> So this is America.
> This is society, in the flesh.
> Attached to tech and broken spirited ragged, suits
> slick hair slick shoes, there is youth and the old who clamp to
> the good old days which is overall the same, oh you fight your
> independent battles over phone calls at night, lights showering
> in a rained haze of convoluted mixed messages of memory
> repeating last night I saw a man buy himself a pack
>> of cigarettes and walk out the
>> gas station I've seen that too many times to know
>> the differences and it'll happened tomorrow and I'll
>> be out in some poetic trance hopping along in
>> thought with feet shuffling against concrete earth
>> rise up to curbside hey you are beautiful,
>>> always.

Not a story to write down.
I expect too much of myself forever and I

see something great in me if I could just rip it out
and give it away to anyone,
               to anyone at all.
I see something great in the world today,
    swallowed in mire and flooded with ashes of
      humanity's decadence deriding from the fold
        of greed and power hunger driven puppeteers.
I see something great in the world today,
      stuck in the back alley slow to death in the cold
        of the big city night!
I see something great in the world today!
 Covered in rust and living alone in solitude with mother nature
                attempting to break free!
    BOLD! BOLD!
      Bold is the truth that dares to dance loose and savage!
      Bold is the love which signals there is unity after all!
      Bold is the hands which rip out this greatness inside and
        feeds it out with only a smile and not a care!
It is the life!
It is the way to nowhere old!
    This butterfly is NOT symmetrical!
              Fluttering in the wind over buildings in our eyes
           attainable yes our consciousness elaborates with
              steel teeth gritting in warm disaster!
Follow through,
Follow through,
        There is nothing
         yet I see forever.

Follow through,
Follow through,
        The shakes and withdrawals
        do nothing but
          slow the heartbeat
                down.

Crash

As the sun sets,
    Without you I have no vision of tomorrow's end.
Today is just today, nothing other than
 today, eternity is fleeting while I
         listen with the junkies
      crash into this morning's rise.
   I have no answers to why I'm moving on.
   I think today is ending after all.

Been given more than I've
 ever asked, and thankful for
 all the love returned eventual to my heart.
A risk the safety of a dream
and learn the truth don't have to sting,
      wailing with the junkies
        crash into this morning's rise.

Gaining Traction

   This light is strong,
       snowed flatlands of Kansas.
   Mountains of Colorado distant behind
     as are heroes of love
          born of noble ideas.
Gaining traction
  against looming emptiness,
      what is said of no clouds
        and people beside themselves in
            their small towns?
    Following 2-cent America,
         bellowing brave military chants
       of spiritual malnutrition,
           zonked out of existence to get
            through existence.

          This lowering sun pushes light towards
            all things,
                  maybe a momentary Heaven,
                  maybe an illusion.

Dough

When the eastern horizon starglo rising, illuminatin
yawning cattle with orange light petting bumbling bovine,
yawning cattle spread upon Kansas
  flatlands reimagined in the new light,
               the new extension,
                       reinvention.
  Peace and assurance begin this day for all.

Rolling, dough hills
      of Kansas.

Pick Up

    Unhealthy,
remarkable breathe steady.
You ain't nothing.
All windows show all no hide.
Agenda vanish waxen skin drip-drip-dripping-drip
    gushing
        juice
        evaporate
as decay sustained trumpet alone
        it dance remarkable breathe steady ohnolosingit.
    We are
    rooted now once more.
        Cut-throat invincibility
            how
    all the
    hippiez cut off
      all their hair.
Yeah, you think
you are but that bus left the station decades
                          a millennium ago and there ain't no
                                coming back.
I would define our culture with
    the image of a limp dick.
Blonde haired limp dick fascist redwhiteblue nationalist green as greed.
How do we?
Do we how?
    How do we how do?
        Do we how now we do how do be itwowza?
    It be do we be we howza wo it wo be do you be it wow wow go be now.

    My chest hurts it clinched I wreck for topsy-turvey
        it be stumble by god xample.

Keep it that keep it tight
tightenupnowwejumpfromviewtoviewofwindow
hidinginforestmythossurroundbighomesandmoneyInothave
andourworldisdistantwithregret Imournfutureusoffutureusnotwhat
wewerewantingbutwegotitandwemustworkwithit,Imeanthekidsare
dyingandmoneysuckedtopeakofsocietytimecollapsefuckinglunacy
moonfreakshowlingAmericancrumbledemiseisnowIweepandprepare
foroncomingwarinevitablepickupthebatandplay
ball.

Neo-Pagan Love Song

        BOMG BOMG
      BONG BOMMMMM
Illusatory fed up good vibrations skills suction and saw chaining tree
to sliced trunk masterpiece I heard how LOVE was made in willowed
mother snickering gunk faces dribbling food and other tasty pastries
crumb and hips pursue body and fuck, yeah fuck to understand the
hands of big god delivering jiving sounds riveting motions looking
at cragged tree and heroes folding capes under dawn of nightlong madness wiping stars from television three colors three dots rearranged and
reconnected to develop images driving for the core nevermind vicious
act and quest accused of hit and run from failure, jaguar lunging for the
food, lioness calling for mane to wake and save the pride dust whirls
typhoon oscillating scared of giant plastic purple revenge riding river of
sadness from New York city bay waters in lascivious hands creased liberty direct point towards mother moon collapsing on whitecapped ripples
emitting fire-red evolution beating down upon the dead weight of love
legalizing puff of forced onward mental sedation pills crushed white
dust mix and end up overdosing on the wrong stuff man fly on little
wings shedding sulking wax hypocrisy to falter and lose gravity defying
limits imposed by feeling pain and by juice of fruit eclipsing modern
needs she and her and the miles between right here in spectral jubilee
kicking half-folded feet in the long strides around rocky mountains
peaked mudded combing through fields salivate heels of your heroic
Achilles sauntering with spear and shield and dead carcass of Hector
son of Priam prince of walled fable now truth Troy mounting horses to
ride away in shame mercy not taken as the Mississippi floods our minds
parachute to survive gold apples refract Jupiter and Mars rainbow
humming birds electric volition navigation own freedom colliding nasty
methods debris grooming young lazy assholes shining with bruised
eyes wishing for the moon gotta get that big cheddar before cat gets
you with incisive claws hooking soul and sinking jarring moans calamity
turn that down but no we keep it roaring fierce punctual feel the

Parker Pickett

beat on time rhyme babby delicious goddess new red shag in the big
garden nursing history and giving birth to seductive sensual sunflowers
reaching voodoo paganistic love songs lunge plunge forfeit your soul in
sacrificial altar upon the mount serpent repent and quick fingers seizing
wild and relentless beauty engulfing unknown spacious digs he swoops
redded amber hair over eyes blued by time and the masking of truth
giggling nomadic fervent being making castles in sand jumping over
fortress of humans dividing all phalanges numbing distorted strange
behavior locked up cream at the bottom of the bottle and rats fucking
in order to survive and cock-
roaches will never be eradicated and the poor strung out hookers limp
on outside under massive uplift magic glow of filled to brim moon each
crater fit within the balance of furious yapping finality creeping as each
bullet in the alleys tonight hushes my demons and raises my neurotic
heart through my throat and sugar cubes dissolved by bright stoic
lunacy residue scent on moustache it is yuck and telephone demands
chatter but we have let go of social progress by demanding to destroy
stupid and repugnant social games ignite flames and thunderhead
whooping song around world succumbing to blaze irrefutable evidence
of fever and sleeping off the disease viral dance to cosmic trajectory
never again to
return and figure out the meanderings of love/
                                                adjacent to you.

Three Days

Three days burning and blew out fuses tripped and stumbled along
 breakneck pace fizzled to dust last night.
Three days spinning fingers and eye sockets lack of care for resting
 pausing leave reality behind not real anyway.
Three days feel overdue to a gasping chance to sizzle out or continue
 the fade but this hyperdriven combustion on nothing more than
 pure choice to loosen control over self has evolved from strewn
 about messages and castrated barbaric emotional guidelines to an
 eloquent and peaceful reassurance that I am not dead and this
 soul is not dry and how I love to lose control when needed,
 within the safety of the boundaries that imagination redefines.

Remember,
energy is not created or destroyed,
    it is give and receive and give and receive.
Give to receive,
receive to give.
               Steady the pace,
               life will balance out.

4:28am in Pittsburgh

Passages of yellow blue white dotted lights carve lines
   in dense block of mechanized urban sprawl.
Come forth from leaning wooden light posts you rats
   scurrying along curbs to hide in grime gutter drains.
Praise be the glory cutting through earthly night,
   triumph of man over nature.

Yet man still dies under the dotted lights,
   yet man still starves in urbanized block,
   yet man still does not remember himself,
      lost in games implemented generations ago.
How big can we become compared to life itself in entity whole?

Facets exist reflect from windows, towers seemingly eternal,
   staunch, massive over populace clinging to hierarchy of
   man-made mountaintops. A sparkle up at peaks reveal
   lifetimes current and past, all imagined cyclical future.

It is now 4:28am in downtown Pittsburgh bus stop,
   Allegheny and Monongahela fuse, export rust Ohio,
   good water, dotted sparkle atop reserve of solid ink blue,
   early morning stillness shrouding little towns,
                 haunting big cities.
Yet hearts still die
   in the still of the night,
yet hearts lose beat
   in the cacophony of society,
yet hearts give out
   when there's no where left
                to go.

Winter Appalachia

Grey bearded Appalachia,
   winter suits your
  felled tree mountains.
 Solitary bird songs echo above villages in the valleys,
                                reverberating.
 Loosen pristine forests virgin to our hands
  remaining free from humanity's sickness.
 Cleansed by sunlight,
   white shrouded farms
     spread weary arms
 hugging this earth in rejuvenating hibernation.

Glitz

Cops fill NYC and
   wind sends burning chills.
Populace packed
   all stepping on each other's feet.
Sender.
Sender.
Sender.
 Not known by me.
Lost upon me.
   Growing stale cig as heat pass
    through bacco stick out of
human face and eyes towards sun,
    reflect off glass towers sun,
      light say no but we go sun.
      And paradise is gone;
        was never here.

    Us fools after fool's gold.

Salt

Cyclical moon white down on New York
 City streets are brutal.
    Homeless man screams
 and beats the salt from his face,
    beats the salt from his face.

Reminds me of America and
 the love I hold for her
    fields extend under blue and bright
    mountains peer across the horizon
 oceans hold this love in place,
    beating the salt onto her shore,
    beating the salt onto her shore.

This is a Poem with No Words

How sheepish my heart and love has been,
unclear on motives within borders I mean imaginative divisions
 contort bodies into
 deceptive angles followed by loss of blood rush to the head flow up fall
 down…
 fall down in eternal frozen river with morning sunshine upon iced teeth.
The population is gone the buildings hostile and charred,
 the future is a myth going back to ancient warlord séances
 in private moonlight recognition leaving truth for ransom and
 secrets for hire
among glowing generations of pat-pattering tight-skull religious zealots
 praising fear of death.
Go join the casket choir in quality jamborees outlining
 satellite societies whooping on the brink of world culture.
Spoonful of ignorance injected through teeth,
 I proclaim the power of the human spirit is strong!
 Having mad and heavy but insignificant strides in
 philosophical meditation on the lyrical mental
 spittings on the early morning roadways going further
 into the unknown America, beyond the roadside!
 Beyond the fabrications concocting beautiful renditions of visions
 obscured through the blurred grainy lens of man's precious
 aspect of time!
 Fully clothed when wanna-be clothed I kinda forget
 that I go day to day looking at darkened and escaping light
 behind the eyes of homeless on sidewalks, sometimes not
 cognizant and other moments the cardboard is their story but
 nonetheless they'll move on as I have moved on,
 as Jesus moved on,
 as Buddha moved on,
 as the bumble-bee found a
 new attractive flower with sweet nectar

A Fist Full of Flowers in the Big Parade

        golden pollen life-creator floating whimsical the
        off-beat state, flat effects of the roads unwound,
        head-under-heels, one sentence reiterated
          by monkey-see monkey-do protagonists dulling the grand
           explorative consciousness that keeps awake stubbed
            records of one human freely expressing
            care for another human,
        all in thy name of self-pity!
I am aware that not anything makes sense
    but I hope to become understanding to the fact that
running in every direction at the exact same momentous
decision to accept the urge creates opportunity to create individual
sense of this life, and with some sunlight shedding clouds and the ocean
waves draining out west with the notion of Manifest Destiny ingrained into
our genetic understanding, the calm release of your heartache and my coy
babbles and mumbles explaining my shy personality I will never
    seem to grow out of,
the affection I receive from concrete whether broken or spray
painted, the old men want that money now now now want control even
though they are sad and delusional, if I could I would die from the beauty
of her eyes as they shudder and gasp and relax with natural
    imperfections which I hold in high regards,
the glow of the city around me reaches to the night
sky, a slate of black chalkboard I wipe off the stars with my thumb one
by one, songs end stories end lives end, but the idea of some grand, silly
   truth to everyone and everything with never die.
      We are born with love for precious life,
       and with that truth I will giggle and smile
        until I'm laid to rest in my sweet,
                sweet grave.

Fangs Aggressive

Growing soft-bodied.
Mind formulating.
Nature turning.
Continued starvation.
Malnutrient spirit.
Poetic relapse.
Caved in mouth.
Future is given up,
no such thing.
Animalia breathtaking.
Stolen from a book
bent from war
twisted in peace.
Casualties mounting.
Bury 'em neath grass.
Blistered driving.
Long-distance dreaming.
Time who cares
when there is no such thing as god
and this great American beast
flexes its fangs aggressive,
croaking frenzied agony
barking mad at you
ferocious in the unsheltered night.

A Fist Full of Flowers in the Big Parade

Monuments (Written in D.C.)

I.
The reigning blood-toothed madness of America unfurls with
tear drops functioning sweat bursting out fresh pores now
heads seething mortal loneliness, spare me avenues wrought
with streetlights and traffic beams and young women stranded
in parkways with no hope to gallop and receive comfort as wind
mashes between buildings enshrined by pseudo-native tongue
snaps, don't listen, I'm your average broke poet on the verge of
    concrete and sunflowers.
This is the head of America, Lincoln's marbled eyes swirling,
    nightscape implodes static secrets echoing police sirens
    wailing other dimension we accept as society.
Stand tall you America,
    teach me how I can stand strong just as you say you do, hypocrite.
Teach me how I can be blind, neurotic stereotypical hatred
    crusading in melodramatic verse,
    calling on the way she walks!
Thick buildings impose pressure while walking sidewalk,
    such visions overlapping constant daydream nightmare state
    of lucid minds holding together despite unequal distribution of
    fantasy and reality, hands fade into pocket seven dollars.
Good business suit people office attire file outside thick buildings,
    hearts compress spirits repressed, no dignity.
I loss of dignity as well, wriggling message on the midnight hour
    ticking folded head of the great American night.

II.
Open air refresh loose sunlight drip through slits in clouds grey and fluff,
suits move luggage
rags limp bags
and bell rings loud.
    Bell rings three times as I sit under tree Capitol Building behind me.

Parker Pickett

                    Where are your monuments?
  Far off other lands?

                                      In your pocket?
The America forces you disrespected life,
    we indulge disrespected life.
And with legs swollen, seven dollars monument in my pocket, I become
peace on the steps of social state, people flocking, cawing for
    photos to share.

                                I'm there but I won't quite listen.
What happened to freedom at large?
Not quite here there outside inside however I can't fathom this moment
or the pain in my legs from stumbling about, I can't fathom where I am,
lively memories do part ways-
      (THE BELL RINGS LOUD AGAIN)
                    —do part ways as I am here shocked in confusion.
The rust streaks from lion's granite maw,
history showing up where the future of America is chosen.
Go go, say what the America is,
high on concrete systems and low on sunflower auras,
bash around buildings singsongy bluesy poesy, cameras
in everything wanting to know our intentions, desires.
    I am where I am who I am survive,
      and the bell rings loud once more.

III.
Buses rubber round roll people bound shoe shuffle
hourglass soothes hippie dance mantras using tongue
to taste earth and sky.
        No why.
        No how.
Broken curbs, bottles shards glass green,
walking non-stop and there floats destiny,
        forever up ahead.
The things humanity has created metaphysical with heart, mind.
What created physical with hands, materials, power, kill.
Finger paintings line sky and one message to another,
                one message to another,
subtle insurgency of poetics divine

and poetics sublime follows hands,
             follows sands,
             follows forever destiny
         through ratrace streets under thick building sighs.
To escape or relate,
         my head dissolves with no-name America.
What now oh golden lands out yonder dream realized humankind
         seductive coastal waters upon the Western shore?
Witness to the carvings of humankind starving for reason in
    reasonless existence
             as history repeats itself day before day.
Nomads of the head,
  there is only knowledge for you.
Nomads of the streets,
  there is only truth for you.
Nomads of the heart,
  there is only ephemeral love for you.
And heartache will not do enough under statues of men
  long abandoned to afterlife and at last, forgiveness.
In tremble hands of America are palms which scoop and cradle,
         with feminine comfort and masculine force,
they scoop and cradle the ebb of consciousness
floating along backroads and small towns and big cities,
everything leads to the big cities. People do not explore
our worlds in virtuosity or valiance against line dividing the now
         and what brings about structures temples castles
         erected to abstain the strain of imagined time.
Oh holy tree above me centered legislative acumen,
         I rest this mind, wilderness has evolved.
What is considered wild?
My bruised feet in soft earth,
I accept and embrace the human division;
             concrete/sunflower.
                 Fleeting and gone, gone,   g o n e ...

IV.
Another shadow in the fold, senses do not sense presence of body.
Along wall I keep to self, populace grow slow to a trickle.

The balance of society has a natural design marred by our idiocy,
                              glorified by our bravery,
                remembering reassuring success of a nation.
    What is success?
    What is excess?
Female faces I can imagine as males when I look at them,
male faces I can imagine as females when I look at them,
faces young I see future creases and wrinkles from a lifetime of emote,
faces old I see rejuvenation childhood coming to rescue damage of
   a hardy life,
      these faces all the same.
What do we choose to preserve and why do we choose to preserve it?
You and I will one day die, my friend.
The America we know will die
     and become renewed,
     just as it has before.
                      Silence the sirens!
                      Open the gates!
                          Give feathers voice to chirp and sing!
                      Our own language holds us back!
Sweeping concrete sidewalks with half-shoe-no-socks-no-teeth
                      medicine man-all-get-mighty
                          with the new age low!
Is life fulfilling the way now lived?
To die quicker?
Sunlight the answer?
Sunlight wrapping 'round stone and metal and fluff clouds and
   populations millennia,
     how ancients spoke mystic mythos emblazoned campfire magic,
     respoke eternity over and over and over and…
It's the end of another day,
It's the wake of another face,
                              pull humbled monuments out of pocket
                              with hands raising, sending monuments
                                  towards the starburnt sky.

Sculpt

    Rich vermillion cut block diagonal blue.
    Arch of rainbow orange sculpted oval.
    Vital green patches cupped light emitted over
              right shoulder and warm enough
                  to steady thoughts as jagged as jazz.
    Wiggle line dragging fanning and wash,
slender umber carving up and laid on top a golden jade
                    loose reach shadowed forest mythos,
              backdrop clean burst of new brick
              and sky hovering to reclaim our wonder.

Post-Partum

      Ripe belly
       fluttering dance,
    nourished affluent chemicals
      melding hormones,
     tunes of arpeggiated swells
   shapeshifting deluge symbolic
     of wondrous revelations,
   nucleus sliced in half layered
texture of light symphony
meekly twirling play with
     highlight stroked hair.

Born bare-backed uncouth merciless
     stretched and yawned from
       delivery neglected by massive hands,
    trembling in dismissive wave,
     shoo-shooing romance aside,
   juggling cut-throat undertones
       flooding each chamber of heart
   needing to fill such vacant
by the way hectic ceremony
two-cent humble darlings
     buried pagan rites of passage
parting swaying stalks verdant
       fields of corn.

Portrait in Prime of Youth

   You body youth 24 and peaking,
    long browned curling flow locks,
    beard dark fresh trim neat no patchy,
    eyes dilated caffeinated thick amber tones.
  Your frame lean muscles resonate past,
    ribcage most prominent says of poverty,
   energized and delirious figure of self
    correlated from stout legs through limp cock up heart
   beat into sight sent reflect mirror physical,
      an acceptance of stature and of natural pose.
Body, you will fade one day soon.
     But today,
body, right now,
body,
     you are able
       are power
       are almost invincible.

One Smack for America

  I hope you feel your heroin,
   nothing such as you but here we are, swinging.
And big Chicago streets widen the strain.
 Who could guess from a small town, so cheap
 living bigger up here,
  nothing bigger than here.
      Sweet opioid calling thy name,
    watching thou stutter aimless onward,
       ragged devouring on fingertips grime scooped desperate,
         pilfered treasure from all trash.
Dilate thou soul and
expand thou heaven,
         sunken as this bliss becomes
        shrunken under the numbness of
        sedation.

This one is for you,
    America.

Med-I-Cal

Opened fury wagging tail anonymous long walk
New York City habitual paint brush scuffing color.

Bury your wonder.
Bury your songs.
Meet your maker.
Squeeze your lungs.

Wild heaven cornered superstitions,
Belittled arduous reports.
He left gaze when cut corner diagonal bye honey.
Water cover everything right back where
 we came spilt blues on skin canvas
  blank stare coital division hanging around
     expecting too much,
  gonna get med-i-cal.

Led putrid voice through
dried blood, instigate purity of faith,
resting hiway side grasses flowering.
Thinking ugly and stepping heat evaporate.

All cities ascend with mirage and go out with disco.
Advantage nature but only belly rounds and becomes sphere.

Green land,
         blue sea,
full of all things if listening.

Enough Coffee

(She plays in the wrong key piano)
I brisk relate evidence enough coffee pot black no juice
    and if I was younger it would fuck me up—yazzuh…
(sharp trill incisive within ear doldrums resuscitate)

        All mornings grafted from
         new birth rhetoric;
                again? Well, I guess.

I warned none,
 so I left.
Walking confusion
 bound by meat
     light and
     skin,
all wrapped and tied by
    a perfect bow
        (smile)

We Went to War for What?

On the friction present
devolving rapid denouncement
here we hang limp and disorderly
demented indictment on worldly ways
exposing closed door secrets.
I value wailing guitars
and silent blackwhite films of mars destitute.
Counting blessing from a god who has never been
and never will.
Shambles uprooted as we each discover holy ground
trampled by well-worn shoes foot traffic gripping
zagging within concrete jag that we come to
claim love and to know when rust overtakes steel sheen
of our disenchanted American Dream.
Revival of warfare we hussle front lines described
hero this hero that drop one bomb gone
with a finger snap.
Forcing voice to learn new words
in order to explain busted nerves
inflamed with boiling fuming rage
quiet in the darkest days delayed
remorse a fraudulent systemic hate
cut-throat robotics compute toxic fate
nursery rhymes as alibis puerility spoiled
when man erupts in magmatic turmoil
wreckage exacerbated political blunder in miasma of grief
beckon ache
become wounds
carved into
all generations follow.

Questioned

        Torm
        ent descend wh
                oo   h
                    az
        credulous disbelief
              ??
      ?Sworn to pro vide
              (tect)
      memories a laugh
         two   laugh
           die   laugh
   answer   laughter
                  , yes
            laughter,
            and in
               tui
                  tion .
                    (?)

Getting chummy now that exchange revelries of words by define slick hair comb out face pockmarked adolescend above past remind when horror of love first no take off underwear slip
      in stretch side jolly nerveshot
        finish quick before
          and that was
            then.

      hahahahahah answered.

Ape Dementia

Youth magnetic beating
the drums of innocence.
Feel hormonal, repeating,
and lash out.
Dry your body it's okay.
Dry your eyes, weeping.
Pulsate on the cusp,
salivate for more.

Fist and bash politico sphere.
Pulled out and slid into
our childhood reimagined,
and in song be primal.
Loosened up and given to
bloom and pollenate,
fruited from the hands of love,
I want to touch your god.

Footprints

        The Dinosaur walks home
           as the sun
          sets but he is
       many miles away.

Big Feet.
Stretch each step.
How old is too old to get home safe?
Locked teeth.
Lift up head.
How old is too old to get home safe?

        The Dinosaur walks home
           as the sun
          down but he is
       running out of time.

Back Home in Indiana

She said she don't like it here.
It what was felt and voiced cleared
 emotion from the stem.
Well here I sing songs of mud and rust,
 of rubble and lust,
 in the flatlands roam our buffalo and
 stories coated crust.
Wounds from opioids let the children cry,
 bedtime lullabies whispered to each ear carrying
 hourly beer don't worry this habit is under control.
I think I met you
 under influence of romantic ideals of rebirth,
 and if I lied because of that I am forgiven and defeat,
 eyes asleep, woke up this morning to taste my
 lovely drug, rolling out of bed to pick myself right up.
 And if I ain't the same as you remember that's because
something had to give in order for me to live,
 remember what you did?
 Stomping in puddles captured by potholes?
Glorious in this rain shifting colors decreased hue
 and emptiness in all this space. I can talk to clouds,
footprints between cornstalks and needles pressed in
 gravel parking lots. I don't believe in fairy tales but
I do believe in magic all the same.
 Course of politico in nature collide abstract lessons
 of fibrous culture pigmented under
 big ol' rainbow crowning jewels of your bloodshot eyes,
something about 3am makes me wonder and weep.
 Stardust blown into divides.
 Gaps in our speech clearing throats.
 Invisible episode delirium.
How about deciding when and how to die?

What final words?
Where tombstone epitaph? Between fields hidden?
Bold and disastrous raging under cover of stars,
       the moon is low tonight and cradled.
 It ain't as cold out here with you.
Pitied by destiny,
   doubled violence in preparation for the kill.
Practiced snapping fingers to keep a beat on silence
    yet this wind is still here pushing childhood along
       out into distant emptiness, where there's room to grow.

A Paper-Cut Will Feed You

Hangin' around some upside down railroad,
    leftover voices spin and grow cold.
It's all a fantasy,
        I say,
lose my pants for
        gravity's sake,
swimming without an
        oxygen tank,
you aren't as dangerous as
        you might think.
While I'm listening through thin drywall
she's resting eyes on Picasso's cheeks,
filling up the square room with square thoughts,
started cutting corners it's a habit at least she tells me
someday she'll decide to live through midnight,
        aren't the stars nice?
    And I wonder why I'm growing up
      thinking in dissonant sounds.
A paper-cut will feed you
a paper-cut will feed you.
Body gave out on side of road.
Hunger strike with no control.
  Easy now I have no feelings for you.
  Graffito blur on the trains passing through.
I can hear her cutting corners in her sleep.
    Oh how I relive it,
      every night.

The Art of Pouring

It ain't the same,
coveted passage safe,
 sound dynamic undulation lines wiggled
               and something occurred.
  Product of sky and of kisses blown.
 Cross winds voyage unto new lands.
Smooch etched into thin flesh cheeks rosy goof.
 Shy blush for evolution of social patterns.
Chipped rocks to refracted ideas
and motions foaming primordial steam.
       The birth of cool,
               of hip radicals stomping wild embalmed
               in haze pulse up through grated gutters
               with night clean vibrant alive calling it
           what the fuck it is.
    Reminded by soft-spoken heroes
   calm pristine inside chaotic free-will
 burst from comatose hypnotic spectral hummm underlying
                             all things.
To radiate then silent.
Folding up voice gone.
Dissolve into acidic atmospheric cushion
       until heavy
         and fall.

Sun Made Us Blind

Oh good lonesome bend of hand structure spastic,
 drizzle your eyes fleeting graze of bovinity,
stress fracture but no worries fill in with nutrients
and worship spotted blotted craze of staring too long
   at sun cindering corneas all that is visioned,
 slander breath value lineage blood lingering
 a sickly green so marred by self-destruction,
                                         yah.
Staring too long at sun wick light flame wiggle chem trails
 path follow breathe expel palm crease loosened
 bend of flame structure alphabetized except word is constrict.
Animality growl velveteen lavender love tones in
 friendly reminder, grumbling to keep fresh,
 morning I thought this was night,
interconnected visage of sun made us blind
so much so missed moon in silver crescent glory humbled,
 no sleep for the weakened, jealousy inverts friction
developed out of close calls pressed phone numbers and
   messages and shut off hey no money,
                  hey,
                        no mon-
                              ey,
as she latches up her shoes yellow sassafras vintage pressed
 between old book pages peeling explanations on yesteryear
 in ahistorical concept realized that life mends even after
 we spread disease.
What do you mean scourge of god?
 Listening and creature no remark?
Gills flap below surface light explores only so far until darkened.
 Same with sky and damn sun gone again so quick but no moon,
 am I delusional always?
Mess in chest pure design exchange punctuation fitting alignment.

Parker Pickett

Gross misinterpretation live in addiction commercial confuse dilated,
teeth hair unkempt girl savors girl excuse me,
more of a reason I allude.
With foot step swinging goofballed round country,
  intrude on altering physical séance wrapping interconnectivity,
            cute bow knot.
You call that scourge of god?
 Priorities fucked skewed I reckon and a sigh pausing
                Fountain Square overpass lean,
 watch traffic lights red motion, same yet differ to beacons peak of
 windmill fixtures rotate, same town discuss same insanity no purpose.
This my brother's love in chaos.
When she eviscerates humanity and good free-will and self-sacrifice of
 lonesome man two-legged relearn walk and
this my brother's love in chaos.
 No moon howl just swig and forget.
  Moving on and mean it, man,
        he means it.
Fresh cut you beautiful son of a bitch!
 Low-life freedom in mattress stained uncomfortable hand-me-downs
 bought from friends of friends lastly residing now in abandoned home,
 turn lot in center of rust-town caught ensnared in days of yore,
 when steam press steal into vehicle choose your color varied hue,
        he means it.
Fresh cut you beautiful bastardized by
 smug celebratory damnation evolving by sunlight stroke
 on window sill, romance in that thought.
 Culled yonder restless waves squirming attrition
 do not decide for him and do not fight for him,
 cursed passages of clothes wardrobes enrobed and
 flowed as showed to demote metaphysical bass lines
 hiding in shrill of personal misconduct, explore destiny
 ripened lobe of fruiting global mystery and woe,
    solid as a stop sign
      in your face and screaming.
   This my brother's love in chaos.
Youth relentless a characterization exclude my manners as such
 frivolous conditions supersede enamored propulsions,

A Fist Full of Flowers in the Big Parade

lifted to weightless vestibule and surrender to uncontrollable
 forces acting upon his body attached to his soul,
  listen and get silent.
 Bobbing and woofing dust trails expansive harmonized tune
 up and get it in just there, sweet spot,
  he means it.
Clear perspective his hunger rampages with demolition scaled down
 to personal exorcisms, hey we all got our own problems, man.
It is this table scattered with useless mail and glue sticks and flowers
 genetic purple and flowers plastic both wilting in unified shame,
  us brothers love the same.
Pausing now to observe reaction, total satisfaction haunting cubist meter,
  balance on ledge
   just
  look over
  no stay you
  step you fall my
  heart oh yammering
  ridiculous banter defiled
  gruesome reflections and over
breakfast what morning my eyes ache bagged out of here over
breakfast seemed frustrated and anger again ain't that the story,
so take a hike brick roads under asphalt expose pulp of the matter.
My brother burdens himself for maternal love he will never quite receive
   and I cannot help save him
   for I have not saved myself.
Feeling of a love being severed and knowing emptiness,
 euphoric pangs of starvation shivering in denial,
  collapsed under another missed moon, sun made us blind,
  shoreline belting symphonic withdrawal from her callous froth,
   boyhood love soured incomplete, yearning still yearning,
   degrading own for any hint of ephemeral specter of maternal love.

It's the way he feels it when he speaks it, man.
  He means it.

Bread and Butter

        Sit inside our ruins.
        I can vision how magnificent it once must've been.
        Pump of steam and exertion of muscle,
        lips opulent with sweat and lofty laughter.
        Bread and butter of capital.

Oh when the stress,
Oh when the stress,
Oh when the stress comes creeping in,
Oh how I'd love to be just another number
   when the stress comes creeping in.

        So, that is where we broke!
        Oh man, hahahahah, no wonder we so fucked up.

Bar neon the groups flock at night to forgo any and all forms of reconcile, pounding down the hard stuff makes a boy into a man,
        makes a girl into a woman,
        makes humanity rot inarticulate.

   Once in
a little while I
see the sunset as
the color of our
   archaic world
     rusting below
plush dark blue sky,
   wasting away in the
   vast universal emptiness
found inside all of us.

Sleep Capsule

    She took the big pill.
Ridges of throat esophagus convulse
and pull pill to tummy.
    Indigestion gaseous fumes belching,
        dismantle chemical make-up of pill,
        dissolve transport bloodstream.
  Go rest your baggy eyes,
      in the other room bed pillow,
    loose sense of awake and body dragged out into slumber.

Put cap on bottle of pills and set in cabinet, cleaning for her.
If only it was that easy to keep up with trainwrecking on every track.
Punished, dared her and she does but wouldn't have it any other
          way.
So turn off tv and drain thoughts own thoughts and allow forces
 of culture and society drag into slumber,
          white noise now
            drags into slumber.

Harvest Remnants

There's no mystery to why rust water clogs the drains.
There's no distance besides what distance to be from you.

Wind locate, sail drag hair opposite,
    barns olden hilltop castles.
In this vacancy these darling moments,
    brilliant juxtaposition.
Contrary to city night life no sleep let's go
    on and on and on until life in debt to stupor.

Warble of chickadee in far off treeline holding
    us back from exploration.
Husk in bloody mud fresh rains soaked in last
    harvest remnants of the lack thereof.

I am too far to remain.
Not the same yet still hopeful,
all along the spirit of change.

Tree Above Farmhouse

You flooding reflection dismayed aberration of web tree.
 Limbs naked canopy, neural network weaving embedding
 roots down into muted earth.
 When the water is the same color of the sky
 and clouds slipping pink sand tones,
triangular center complete stability in wild expansion towards sea.

Spark of passion relayed through wood splintering
 rings of Saturn cream awash the world
                indicative of division
                        of tension
                coddled into armistice.

Womb

    I see the world eat itself massaging
      notorious disasters lugging along
   puny man and his search for meaning in
    meaningless,
      oh conditional folly of us all.
Have multitrax
layered over lathered up
rock metamorphous being
malleable by time
and tectonics, baby.
You know how bodies press upon bodies
     floating on magmatic ecstasy causing
    peaks to stretch fabric of sky.
     Solid audaciousness sweating from clouds hovering in heat.

      There is the goodness of childs playing
       basketball use trampoline to be Kyrie Irving
      snapping fools ankles and driving in to slam one
       in and that is righteous, man.

Been caught thinking too much.
  Sleight of hand?
 Non-state lover?
Paganism? Who knows what that is anymore,
    we all but killed such cultures round these parts.

Come back to me come back to me come back to me come back to me.
Selfish just as your mother is
    bird on branch tree out windo
      windo clean
     red-copper bellied.

Back in recessed images of mind.
Take me home so bad,
wake me up so bad.
I want to drown face-first in mud,
have every molecule of earth wriggle down my throat,
body caked in flies buzzzzzzzzing,
swallowed become petrefied
once again within mother.

Old Glory

      Weaponize masses.
       Leak missiles.
      Napalm bones to glue.
     Desert sands a mockery.
      Fountains of Babylon filled
       with bullet shells and
      tattered rags of Old Glory
      stained by hands grubbing for petrol gold.

We are our own enemies.
Heads lathering lies on rich palette.
Stroking field boys and grooming the poor.
Give you the guns and the smarts.
Restrict to regimental behavior.
Yousa boy playing soldier out in the back yard again.
Rejuvenated by bloodshed
 and crippled by the pyramidal structure
                fueling war.

On Midday Roll

Hey hey the cops pulled to cuff.
Hey hey red/blue pummel her face mashed.
   On midday roll
  crowd street populous feverish
  gotta hear the news
   of what they did to you.

Oh my my,
 obstruction indeed.
Hands up make 'em bleed.
 Eradicate for the purpose of the state.
 The best way to get rid of poverty
       is to kill us,

Where Nothing is Found

You figure out
You no sat
You big ugly
You tremendous ugly
I say I say I say da Bible
I say I say I say FUCK
I say I say I say
  remember his face gotta slope to nose and
  too much tan skin and ears too big to listen
  and eyebrows connected and
  he chews as he spits lavish talk pummeling
  inside mouth cave.
He sayin'
he wantin' die or somethin'
he wantin' sandwich from diner then drop off at
                   predestined grave with
                   no hero journey,
                      ride straight 6ft.
WOAH -breathe between bites!
       Collateral function you know
           monuments yadda-yah let's FUCK for you kno
                 god's will or whatever HAH.
Estranged in delirious dissatisfaction,
mad mad mad I'm baby
       I'M baby
       I'M BABY   (repeat it this time uglier)
       i 'M b A B y
I say I say I say
        ain't that what war is?
   Dumb jargon of front lines pop-pop-pop-pop-pop
    caught in arm wrap it,
   caught sight of nerves jolting it was fabulous

A Fist Full of Flowers in the Big Parade

        never want to give that again.
Return gas station pale light long night drive foolin' between
bold American coasts and raided hope when meshing ego
when dilute and prophesize by way of anger on streets of
              nestled mountain Denver,
              hip fabled Denver,
  where all who dream too big find growth,
  where all who feel the beat find heart,
  dumb Denver goofing in widened avenues wafting pot,
  marinate air in marijuana puffs, eclectic mountain rise.
Fellowship centered round bloodied bruises we
swore off the cold we swore off passion but c'mon,
let us rip out roaring weary gusto into fruited plains!
And the cops will not protect us!
                They will go for the poets first.
                They will slaughter the free spirit.
                They will silence the voice of the people.
                They will go for the poets first.
                They will execute those who defy
                        and all poets defy.

So speak!
So sing your dilapidated heart out dear!
So deliver the message in honest rage and never falter!
  Beat back the culture in furious exposition of melodic verse!
  Report on all subjects in all manners all-ways!
It is coming,
It will happen,
  decadence is all desired and what they want
                      they get.
              Ain't that what privilege is?
                what they want
                    they get,
                    they will
                make sure of it.
Lambasting car horns no news no good news besides I
seeing you and you being happy and I being good, content
and at ease even with bleak horizon chopped by buildings.
  Skipping in rainbow glow of after summer reigns slipped crown

shine gloom now rats and vacancy.
I am of bombed out buildings.
I am of drug fueled self-destruction.
I am of isolation and of where nothing is found.

            You sound older,
           where have you been?

Practicing song and space.
Practicing love and patience.
Practicing both lessons of truth and
  finding path leading towards
   reconciliation of self,
      of this I sing
        for you.

Post-Digital Poet

The old god-head lit some candles.
We've all been waiting, exuberance for exalting light.
A politic hear, a politic there.
Collected sea-shell sand-castles and sculpted our world.
Could've been ordained "masterpiece".
Could've left body agape moon-howling in eternal city alley-wayz.
It was tongue, once bitten, twice lathering language to depart.
A fusillade, emote rage,
 sharpening the tools of war.
Idealistically, I'd die much too much alone.
If luck ever be a lady, she'd break all hearts including her own.
I would find the still pumping pieces to bury them proper,
   traditional pleasantries with ideas of immortality, planted to bloom.

Some way, some exotic day,
 a transcended being will happen upon our artifacts of love,
 existing momentary misty-eyed,
 and evolve.

I Should Have Communicated Better

Deconstruct your constructs.
Detinker your tinker machines.
Play the warble of funny birds and
 the humming-wings of dancing bees.
Pollenate your empty vacant fields in mind,
 sew them with thread of wildflowers erupting
all rainbow spectrum unleashed upon our lands.
 Laying down with face leaning towards
 fragile membrane we describe as
  "sky"
 splitting through to finally speak
  for the first time
   of all-time.

Criss-Crossed Stars

Desaturated blank state.
Echolocate, idiocy revealed.
Peeled oranges spray nectar.
Better her than anyone else.
If legs could spread,
 if eyes could close,
 if resolution finite,
 if radioactive decays.
I hang limp breathing us.

Oh thin heart papier-maché!
If we could crumble and rebuild
  with magic and totems
  blessed by karmic bodies,
 each wanting to untangle
            their stars.

Find Mark Return

How grass cover all,
        so I rest on
           and succumb to relax breathe counting
      measurement length find mark return,
              find mark return,
          beetle walk six leg on wood stem
            and woman grieve loss abandon her lights out
                    door window shut,
          and television off to walk outside they revel.
        We are alive in the chaos of now!
      Ragged madness set me free into new-liberation,
  and the world rebellion quiet decay as hearts distorted by
                    deceit and dismay.
And I am found new-liberation
radical lover of the night elation
patterned truth after what turned out to be lies.

          And youth numbed dehumanized limited stunted,
            and old broken eradicated by times of now they unable
        to keep up to speed,
         and politics doomed I love the flag burning all flags burn!
                  All religions burn!
              All wars burn!
                All profit economo burn!
            Stand and become what is needed!
        In the furious evolution humanity must evolve
            beyond our belief in tech,
          evolve beyond capabilities of the old-age.
        The atomic age is over!
        The world wants a new song!
We tired of that old drag needle around grooving discs,

we tired of the mediocre playlist jumping no destination no end
                              no finish,
we tired of all those parrots yupping up to the
  big-mouthed mothafuckas masticating on dogshit.

            We know what the fuck has been going wrong, man,
              quit lying to yourself and quit letting lies
            seep into your sub-conscious train of thought, man.
Sink back, remember how you were born?
Screaming exhausting wails.   Chaotic brutal love.
              And all was new.
    And the only thing you could do
    was watch in wonder and soak in such love,
                        given to each of us to one day
                          be returned just as easy
                            as it was to arrive.

Crystal Orchard

I don't know where this came from, nothing of sickness
and how we age appropriate to each spatial object defined
by set lines connecting at points,
what I was told by George at truck stop restaurant while hitchhiking
    up hiway,
he mulled about crystalline structures and how the molecules
are aligned, separate yet they are still connected, whether momentary
    rigid or
liquidity vibrates us as we slide further apart, always interconnected.
    I understood him.
    He elated moment wholesome glow his eyes.
    Good light, orchard George.

He is dead now.
He was killed in
someone's front yard one night.
He was shot up bullets.
I do not know the reason
nor does it matter,
 he is gone.
Along with mystic speak,
 he is gone.

We are still connected,
 even if only by thoughts, memories of supple realizations.

An History Resurface

   Illicit strength,
  pinky-sized lip-stick-red flowers
bloom from vines a seductive green
  and an history resurface,
feelings are quite difficult to shake.
    Maybe now a bit wiser
   and more complete and said of
    strength in tiny flower,
well,
     how 'bout strength
          in tiny you?

Barriers

There is sacred love within you
working madness for passionate thrust.
Bigger than Montana within you
 and blue skies weaved by jet stream.

> You have free-will,
> choose to use it.

It is Demanded that You Grow

Nestled in undergrowth swallowing rooted hymns
 revolve axis storied by all-time silent green
  cupping below leaflets spreading from sapling shells.
Split wide raw beat red grasping shudder heart attack.
         Suck up the earthen song.
Widened honeyed pot filled life,
  teeming organisms vibrate stationary.
 A veil of life and our stasis in innocence
              or perceived innocence.
Fierce red lather over gold daffodil, moss eaten bark of
 society construct peeled off left to decompose.
A haze creep above mist foliage sopped veins
 pumping pursuit expel oxygen so breathe,
              yes, breathe.
Under us and our imaginations are the bright wings
 of little heaven keep afloat mystery and curiosity
 to reveal what is inside each of us, figure our environment,
 your eyes bushy flutter hide as best as possible such reliance
 on this embodiment of prime existence.
Motion life of commotion the tiger stalks chaos push through
 purple a royal pain bludgeoned into meat into sight swirl
 cyclical calamity red hot scythe slip ease through orange
 pollen delivered sing for radiance of birth.
Seismic conclusion thump of big-bellied beat keep rhythm
 on demand whip whip, it is demanded that you grow, that you
 sick curious be resolved and fix for passion fed undiluted experience.
Coral flower lesions drip in span of exotic universal drag wearing away
 at the teeth when steal vitality from superior sap, long slithering lap of
 love berating hormone institutions, you struggle on color wheel.
Outlines of figures escape physical momentum, jealous betray,
 count each day as each leaflet spread land light exposed by intensity
 and by fabled destiny criss-crossed as constellations rearrange and

the whirling revolutions of Earth slow and we remember, surrender.
Clean wiggle neon cascade through center pouring on in afterglow delight,
 pooling to be revived in hallowed song awash in sprayed consciousness
 rainbow mist, purpled eyes bawling want to open up and love,
 folding roll delirious magic shelled from monstrous storm raging,
 deny the way we choose to die in vivid sleepy communion arching bliss.
Tessellating rose petals, all energy recycle vortex precise and fluid
 soaking in completion, wondrous belief in voice.
A defiance of death resolved in as close to complete life
 defined in mother's colors saturated to the bones.
Feeding from the marrow and you float sincere,
 to and fro violent despair into reclaimed ephemeral purity.
All in all a simple return to your birth.

Wail

Backseat love culture.
Off radar know-alls
  limiting and stunting hedonist answers to undisclosed obligations.
White aggression fueled by fears and emotional manipulation;
  there's no such thing as "control", there's no such thing as "country".
Congrats on reappearance of doomsday clock countdown,
  bitter flavor a charade masking feverish licks voice limping
  enraged and seduced by megalomanic veneration,
  depleted umph propelling kind balancing fools
  repulsed by retroaction of American culture.
   Religion archaic
   Politico detached
     Socio faux
   Economo rigged
  Communicative pilfered
     Relation hampered
Climate sickened
  Cities under skin infectious,
      each road intertwining fabric tattered pot-holed.
No mercy under fucked flag of a jingoist narrative
        primed by evil men hunting every single free-tongued brave poet
  venturing in ideas warring with contagious dissent
                warring against current modern symphony.
(Yo yo yo play a different tune, this one sucks)
        Overt in pride, get your shoes on get your feet up glide on over,
              give your self a name.
  Jostling sounds, patterns rhythmic,
     declare how free you are!
         RIGHT HERE! RIGHT NOW!

(One long wail on through end of existence,
        direct into beyond.)

Look Momma

>   What's this mean for the kids
> in America?
>   What's this mean for the kids in
>   America?
>   Hush up.

WE got a big world dying look momma no hands when I clap and to
nothing we devolve monsters under beds we calamity riding fearsome
toothed sn-arling after wake momentaryjubilate jewel of coastal waters
cleanse burdens and foment aggressive swoons kicking out of time
keep upstroke the menacing fueling happening happenstance wicked
gnarly egregious loops of atmospheric vindication moreover folly of
human soul freak ignite gotta subtract your messages from the prompt
young and lively usurping hero quiet you hero ignoring strands of
future fate reconcile on the afterthought of ruined love and murdered
opportunity velvet blue robes reduced to smeared gunk crashing
doorframes exact revolt huggin mention of alabaster face wind howling
ricochet buildings taller than what eyes will perceive especially now that
we have our failures known contained in our grasp reluctant and have
mercy on us yes on us do-good people never limping or slaughtering
or exacerbating lyric lathe reduce syllabillic estimate worn out beau-
teous tangerine skin peel oh you are the apple of my eye red adorned
with leafy emeralds postulating fervor in a dying land sick to bones
stacking bones on top of hills decaying inside out we are decaying
inside out and last will be our eyes that will glow sad lavender hues as
we watch the fall of all that we know sub-conscious dear to our mortal
hearts withdrew battling invertebrates to risk the memories of eden
of goldmines littered about the mind earth magnetism positioning
and love strangled by choice to lose such empty near-narrow-minded
feeling power over simple exquisite murmur chipped paint on worldly
walkways licking legs no shave feet older they hurt when step I seen
too much not enough valued all of us and the mo motions deciding
gooooooooooooooooooooood humored validation pulsive rejoice I am

A Fist Full of Flowers in the Big Parade

not gonna die empty handed! swear that each plop of rain jostling down from heavens is atonement for dry-heaving madness suppressed by glorious aspect of futile time and pushed far back into thoughts of yesterdays that mean little to nothing when all is said and done man, yeah man, we man human we rolling blunts sucking that good good man, we skip into other dimensions where the boss ain't the old boss and the cops ain't even a thing and blackwhite no matter baby we all poor yet rich in the moment of love communal temple adequate reflex of gullible green asphyxiated into orange radiance overlapping mountains and folding all we wondrous deified into surrendering sleep, yield to the calls towards freedom, liberation vivified by talk and by urgent decay, hey also, when you walk the walk you must talk the talk and if you talk the talk you must believe in something other than futility in the dormancy of radical thought…..?

> You got a face too real for phony magazines.
> Yeah yeah I've heard it all before.
> Chewed up my shoes our cities repeating.
> If there is anything better more wild than this.
> Coaxing pleasant vitality within infinite space.
> Politics no gods, books no gods, religions no gods.
> Put your ear to the timbre of the wind, translate into song.
> A voice as fatal and as beautiful as standing on the shores of looking back from the shores of limited existence.

Masticate

Lost all power.
Plugins no use.
Decided to flower.
Petals draped refuse.
Shade has charm and history.
Menace of July where winter is dying
 and snow is extinct now.
But the days are short
 and we celebrate holidays alone.
Counting beats per second,
 coming up with the ocean tide
 pulverizing speech patterns.
Carry the scent of shotgun.
Blowing out candles left and right.
Chemical reaction propelling vision.
Sometimes things do not work out.
Flesh torn apart tendrils hang limp,
 body stomata created by man.
Lost all power.
Devour seclusive hate.
Lying awake at night to walls hostile white.
Clamoring wetted cheeks beauty in suffer.
Nuisance of breathing, in the way, get out.
GET OUT.
Cold-cut right through, no bullshit.
Chest ripple muscle tighten.
Imperfection guiding delivery.
Celebrate holidays alone.
Broken heroes taking out trash to back alley wind gushing look up sky
 powerlines collect social filth reminisce shoeless withdrawn.
Solipsism amounting to fool sorting emotions.
Fuck and send.
Vermin now opulent.
Pick teeth clean and shine.

Pull My Daisy 1959

    Figurative paint meta walls white round table door open
early morning in the universe.
        Paint rail brakeman,
   Kimono neck ties socks kid to school.
Poor Pablo, knock is beat.
       Got drinks and poems put a match on it
   goodbye, swing in streets Empire doom building,
the struggle of poets.
          Gum chewing geniuses.
     Tight hats wash face for bishop hang up
  acting saint all saints
   air through pipe flute nonsense,
couch messages face is soaped
    going back to Venice.
      Welcome dance those steps and feel free!
It's these poets meet!
    Mother, take your gloves,
  piano staggers,
wants that tea oh bishop not right time mother
   goofing, serious all of us.
Are we in heaven now we know it dress pulled to length,
  ignorance rippling above doves agree case in point.
Think about anything,
   white suit among black angeled haloed stepped organ
bing-bang-dopp
       gang growing step around woman feels good,
   know nothing say something,
       baseball girls tight dresses holy
  and the hippos were boiled in their tanks.
Boys cowering under covers lines bleeding too much into
  paper and to
    and from
    and lengthened telegrams paired by
  echolocation.

Parker Pickett

Ring-ding-sing-sin
        won battle after battle
  christened new loves,
all the world has changed already
but now this language is in session,
salivate gravitate excommunicate from churches-
        global church
        pope church
        city church
         family church
        dog church
          road church
      war church
        politico church
            socio church
        economo church
    church of thy everlasting self!
Inhabiting vibrato nuclei
        cells tuned in B minor (bee my-nor)
            F sharp (eff shh-arr-puh)
    Poor boy born in a rut and
      now that rut is worn out,
        need a new drag new bacco stick.
You know that Buddha one way not other not
wicker chair silver ladder mumbling white men brooding
  quiet place knows what talkin bout
  ministers of the line oh daddio,
    disturb midnight evening buddy on toilet
   by god the woman feels good,
hands go around shake introduce evening in dilapidation.
  I don't know anything,
    what I really mean,
teeth worn hold flag preach is cold and glasses refract
 singing group of wild silence over-heads universe
    sucker out of mouth cave of sherried heroes
glazed up,
      rocking with the port taken and discussed
silly friends
  slaps to face and all in bathtub

A Fist Full of Flowers in the Big Parade

rinse dishes roaches roaches tribal drumming
        coffee pot
mirror is dancing finger guns.
                Young people strange,
  world holy bishop holy mother organ music
Peter, give me the chair!
    Dust off the pillow
 come and pump for me!
             Comb your hair
            stay up all night
       roll over in bed and figure what is holy.
Puffed cheeks brass sounds,
   mother go on home,
        doing something and saying goodbye
gotta leave
  sit on my lap quit your sleep play my horn,
      see those notes see that dress?
Little Pablo
       pequeño Pablo
             little smoke.
  And they 4 do something they've never done
       Pakos country dusty wino preaching with gun

POW
       All this nonsense fed food give give did
         nothin' no understand poets play by fires,
            Don't cry

MILO!
      Don't cry.
            Rose swings,
            she'll get over it.
  Off they go
        the boys fly in the big city night
     off to find adventure
  as the rose swings till morn,
  as the
      rose swings
          till morn.

Here We Indiana

Everything has been easy today.

                It don't make no sense.

Gabions relent, pacifiers of descent,
spread out all our love is on the floor.

Hiways of mid-heaven, each car patting other vehicles
on the back, engines hummm alongside breeze midday,
sunlight warmth frayed hair, mechanized rollers
                      strolling out yonder St. Louis
                      and Louisville from
                here we Indiana front porch of
                              the world.

Kingdom of Daisies

I've been breathing all my life
wind gushes wails scatter with delusion.

Fingers press for frequency of laughter
ripples of ribbon gasping beneath spoiled sun.

Anger expressed lauded with grief
while history of granite explains desires of social code.

Dawn of a new age of input belittled by output
wiped tears with digital numerals sent by electronic gasps.

Myopia seems to be what is bred into most
haunted by déjà vu reintroduced as the current the now.

Flavor packets colorize old wounds
streets outlined by legal jargon limiting discovery.

Hand clinches when she walks unsteady
flowers adorned gold rooted in black health thrive.

Search in through window from outside where the world waits
to rescind casualties mounting on all frontal lobes dangling.

Teeth bent 45 degrees grinding to a halt sudden
lean on buildings towering malicious demeanor on every able bodied.

No gods no heavens no immortal sans passive questions
quipped as good cities putrid and jaws gape aghast.

Disorderly life paces on into constricting web of time
where birds perch on powerlines tying together telephone poles,

exhausted where the nowheres of exist connect and bring
about new visions rising from scars of a world wrought death.

How about that new melody?
Swinging beat change of key,
idyllic slumber leave me be
to resurrect my king-
dom the shine of daisies.

Rome Wasn't Burned in a Day

>Are you big enough to let the world die?

Easy does it,
 not meant for the pastures munching mild somber skies.
Comb out wooly silent curls, not the same start.

Bunching up a few rails of coke,
    pack in and roll,
 ain't high enough yet.

      Kids flailing decomposure.
     Stained carpet, flickering.
  Only getting higher, S.O.S.
   (It is all-right, man)

>Maybe work to simple, non-shape definitive.
>Lemon yellow grin blushing, what?
>Overachieve body limit and suck,
>   people laugh good yesssss I want
>   laugh in utter confusion.

Exposed?

I got a cold heart aching to be burning again.

Coffin buried under tree metropolis reclaiming earth.

Example:
 One rock picked up hewn shatter glittering spider web glass.

Exposed?
 They glimpsed softened post-coital cock through her window she
 nightgown follow my path she wanted any cock so bad and
  called mine cause ease and pleasure.

I got a cold heart fanning crackle-flames wanna burn
                                                red hot.

Our city wilting night's out over turn off busy get to slumber.

I ain't mean nothing by it,
                by us.
Any developing attrition is rumination of boundaries and
                desire to shatter boundaries
                        said ruminate.

Exercise:
 Get off get out stop kissing shut up fuck me harder cum please
 cum you aren't special yes yes YES!

And if we leave it be?
Would even dull birds warm their beaks to sing?

I warble winding willow-hearted
contagious she blockade emote remote

no-no, what fear of vulnerable
has seized, she thinks she has control.

Oh boring lies one day drowning boat of love capsize
    and if not for me,
        so it be.

        So it be.

Big Brute

America, you big brute
I no salute you I no salute.
I shake in hunger in debt,
no fortitude in debt.
No money no food no empathy,
in debt.

America, you sinister salivate
and devour self, so starved
begin to tear at own flesh,
consume at self; nothing
else tastes as sweet,
as loaded-up preservatives,
as far removed from
reality and nature.

Cave Paintings

        I tore at the shrubs searching for where you stand,
      flipping out and sick victim no no no fooling around shout out
shout out from heaven and quit your demon squeal.
  Lunatics all patient so we wait for an end or something,
      who knows?

        Eastwind tumbling west,
      the northstar flocking south,
        tied my shoes to my hands
      and opened up my mouth.

Nothin's wrong
Nothing's wrong don't you worry.

        Practiced Armageddon
        lighting up the sky,
      gulped from the spring of truth
      and whispered only lies.

Nothin's wrong
Nothing's wrong don't worry.

        Fortified my haunted head,
      took pictures of all ghosts,
      petrified the sun went back
          and the world's in comatose.

Deciphering while wide awake paintings on cave walls
showing man hunt and run beasts off of cliffs to extinct,
this how we kill all beasts.
Nature tells us to jump,
              it is our turn.

Monkey Losing Fucking Mind

Contained the blues gurgling knowledge on soul.
Long-haired freaks gotta carve out songs.
Scrape words and notes in arms while widdling away stupidity.
Cowardice when punish by nashing head and puncturing gut.
Wicked worry everlasting.
Longer than silence which is eternal.
Hung love on an upside down cross made from welded rust beams
  (more beautiful that way).

I step out from mouth of cave
 fitted by furs and hunger.
Jostling teeth from beasts felled in egocentric behavior.
Just trying to survive, so exclaims.
She said yesterday she hated.
She ran out of pills to crush up line up and suck.
Monkey see monkey do monkey losing fucking mind, man.

20$ in bank gotta make that last a whole week or more.
Cleaning piss off of tile and off of leg.
Gimme something to puke up I wanna be thinner.
I wanna be humiliated.
Floating on low heat coals gaseous glow red outlined by white ash.
Intimidated by shadows deceived by trauma.
Pressing diamonds rage pressure absolute yelpings accumulate mutilation.
We celebrate by burning down all churches.
Where we are there is no such thing as god.

Observe the Evidence

Invincible yard schoolkids absent no yelps bellowed across equipment
a fraction of forever reside and bask in self-allegiance,
 saw off otherworldly a satisfactory individual
proclaiming nothing but the truth in a period of incessant lies,
trickle-down theorized never felt a single plop drop down.

>   Guess I am still alone
>   always am I still alone
>   nothing shared nothing whole
>   and each feel fine
>   (and each feel fine)

Took a while to observe the evidence undisturbed 'round yr neck
fashioning bold empire spilling blood to soil and soil to the sun
upon own bodies conscious and alive berating lyrics of tragedy
cropping cream what's between you and me and our country tis of thee
hiding from the slaughter come knock-knock-knocking locked
     chamber doors.

>   Push the war upon our shores
>   Siege our hearts guarded fear
>   Supplant vigor with muddled confuse
>   and each now ready
>   (and each feel fine)

Pouring Out of Hearth

I bellowing beyond the cages of man,
prisoners rattling bars
    clink-clink-clink
   cups of no change,
musky concrete bunkers hiding
disconnected from universal woe.
       I
            force
                voice
                through wall,
blips radio frequencies transmitted by flames pouring out of hearth.
 Raspy smokey voice of uncharted imagination
      calling for you!
        yes,
            you!
Put foot to the stone and GO!
Shake earthen tombs buried for millennia forgotten by all
                besides those who still
                    spit their secrets into the furious sea.
Appalled,
confused,
tally up the hours of dormant behavior,
cruel and unfortunately usual conditions
      padding maddog humankind.
Lips and jowls slobbering furious salivate
                  furious reckoning with collective sea
           sprayed coast to coast.
I listen to the song
swirled within a conch shell,
come out!
      yes yes yes come on out!

You move slow and fresh trepidation,
   sticking mucus from womb trail of slime glistening behind.
        It is okay,
      take your time,
         soak in all you can,
            and grow.

Upheaval

She aeroplane,
    one side dragon, scales magic.
    Interlude in nude lips punching with blonde shine.
    Interesting madness spittle dripping wetted sludge
on forest floor, eggs of flies newly nestled
        batches baking under blossoming flames
          scintillating nostrils with birth rituals
    and a magazine open to interpretation.
   Dialogue and diatribes quoted misdirected,
  zen found in barreness center of USA
when signal through the flames of
our earth teaching us a lesson
      on politics.

Pulsate Within Her

> You hear me calling you our
> just yet feeble attempt
> at veneration.

Woke up and
grey outside
socially acceptable
the function of stagnation
in seducing those who choose to
rot slow in their brains
and stay put.

> She nerve endings and dilated pupils.
> Sensory overload has never before felt euphoric.
> Grandiose verbose valiant song swaying
>   the hearts of young studs flexing their
> muscles and gritting their teeths for a
>   chance to swagger around and pulsate within her.
> Lyric peach flooding juices flood of biblical proportions,
> heating up the atmosphere intoxicating aroma,
>   bodily desires pressed and extracted
>   from each experience of you.

WHAMO!

What will you create of this?
    That's an arm length of side-kick love, screw.
  Needle bed, ridden, gallup from newer horizons, fresh sunsets
                                  are not to be
                                      met with regret.
Emboldened with finger gun (weapon of choice)
          click
          point-> === WHAMO!}
(scream)
       [pretend this line has no words…]
                                "I never thought you'd
                                leave me, why?"

Why worry?…….   I'm just
               leaving myself.
                            "You think you're powerless."
Question why door has closed.
Question why teeth don't ache.
Question why store sells you.
Question why no more rulez.
Question why love is free
          except when sold at Disneyland.
Question?
Quest to bathe illuminated knowledge,
       ecstasy of you evaporates soon enough,
      shriveled carcass continue to hold hands.

Mother Fly

You America you gawking unamused,
   floor dirt you eat filth,
  raw meat got hiccups chatter yellowed teeth.
     Bloated on side of road carcass maggot-filled,
         mother fly laid her eggs and went.
       Let the cycle complete itself.

And yes you rain, soak this city flooded,
         carry this cyclical universe,
          a passenger swept by unknown,
       begging pure-rot-rite-of-death,
        you poor bloated thing.

You America you pushing pavement skyward fenestrate,
      add windows add fortune scraping whatever
        gods are believed in, a sacrifice for them.
         Spilled blood a paper-cut.

 Almost king of all creation but thy spirit is
    gone been dead for decades.
   Our populace adrift is pain,
  soothing throat with a sip inebriate,
    block out no speak,
        only beat
          and drive ourselves to a complete and utter death.

Mud Tides

Mud tide fields oversaturated.
 Sky pink tint and masses squirm in order to not drown,
            poking wiggling bodies out of tilled flat earth
          and submerge rows of sproutlings,
             never gonna survive.

Struggle who cares when piling bodies high?
Grieve in lonesome silence as the rains don't
   stop the rains will not stop and
       the mud tides rise past our peaks.

Great Pets

        Have the tongue dog do yes you.
        You have the tongue of a dog, yes you.
        Do you crave with bubbles stack saliva billow
            jowls whimpering efficient excellent?
          Set paw splayed toes remorse
          paw remorse toes set splayed.
              Whimpering more means less food.
              Mongrel scavenging dinner table prepared
                table vulture on haunches.
    Yapp you yapp,
        pilate on skin upright when subtle shift,
        thickened fur vindictive as each second goes without
            sharing of what selfishness retains.

I believe there is
 a street outback where
 in this wide strange America you belong
  adjacent to trash can mounds,
   crawling beneath crushing poverty,
    subject to chemical emancipation
    and the social horrors inflicted
     by those who belch gold dust
      and chortle mockery
       at distorted figures bumbling,
        unaware of a reality
         harvested each day by
          the mechanized odious American greed.

Chatter

  Hugged the coastlines pushing the peaks here low-lit
faces gather to eat each other's romances can one
  say I love you too without getting too close?
  Bashful eyes flutter from flatlands and history tells us
    of what this exit holds.
Dried wounds healed with time and regenerative properties.
Enzymes and proteins built up from defeat and seductive
                    hormonal techniques.
  No longer king and that's okay.
   Buried bent crown and suffocated scuffed scepter and
took fire to velvet cloak and wept out each vicious flame.
    You are a body to touch to hold.
     Leaning against building crumble songs
         resemble and devolve into
         merciless chatter of insects
          dying by the frost of winter,
         exoskeletons flimsy erode
        under twilight of mountains and
        innovation of language,
             of touch.

Do the Math

Two homeless men
ragged concrete bitten clothes
widdling under building shadows
living in their graves
discussing calculus.

Each Strand I Find Splitting

Pulling out hair to keep mind preoccupied with
action while winter inaction pulls heavy on Anderson.

Dragging heat out in snow what else now
it is time to go and left her with her heart
too scared to cry.
    Cannot deny any passion even passionate for pain
     intolerant and scuffed to bones be it so.
Not simple yet swear to be precise in excising
such a demon as death do us part well here
death is a dream and in such dreaming
   I live, baby, counting me out and
    solitude divine ineptitude devise a message
   a song slipping with whistles and hooks
  to get across divides worth fighting
     against and bridging for comfort
     and stability, you smile I
      smile and in due time I'll
     move on and what now?
After even giving up found out it is more difficult than being sold
on such a way to give it all away.
   Moments I am saddened and bolstered by defeat,
    each strand I find splitting,
      just as my heart is.

Valuable Resource

Be applied by ego
and man walked by dog.
Kicking snow here Anderson, Indiana.
Booted to shoot worship
   of higher plain of crops.
      Begging plush
       promises crushed.
  What it is to grow too tall
  and then be taken and used
  for vitality and valuable resource
caving inside of empty home?

No one knows,
and that's fine.

Elvis Ain't Good

Collecting difference of opinion oh great America bully sour with
delight manufacture overlap of language divide for taxes for
financial control and done did release pigeons from streets
fencing buildings and skyscrapers with pedestrian worn-shoe flow
of traffic honking getting in time whatever digging your
shoes made for television glitz and love a continuous form
of reality buttressed by belief inane unsophisticated banter on
unnatural, the celebrated lives unnatural growling, so swing
farm boy rust towards different locale telling tales of
American decay body bumping body cyclical rooted bloom pink
nectar swapping juices with diluted privacy all-be-it I'm just
being a dick and Elvis ain't god.

To Babylon

If you felt romantic
take a bite outta me
one that's gigantic
sharpen up your teeth
no holds against you
no holds against me
ain't no social rule
outside society
burn to smoke signal pile of leaves no fire just pile of leaves
in the woods just a pile of leaves in the streets just a pile of leaves
in the minds just a forgotten land
Babylon is make-believe
Babylon is a pile of leaves
Babylon and Euphrates
Tigris just to the east
sun will rise
just to the east
if you want time
fill the palm of your hands
in the hands a forgotten land
where's our future Babylon?
where's our future fertile land?
golden crescent in our heads
in our minds what is dead?
answer for what you seek
answer for what romance
on your tongue bitten outta me
Babylon bitten outta me
displayed romance on the streets
don't wanna push too much in veins, blowing vocal chords
with sounds inhuman although true and only believable if

swallowed waves with ear, not that close yet oh so near, step
in puddle spilt oil rainbow coating surface, seems vehicle
a little sick, this wind gonna pick us up and carry us all
away and how happy we'd be for at least a little bit, all
that's asked is a little bit, public display I don't enjoy your
rhetoric, seems to make me a little sick, sold the future to fix
              with a kiss
              no tongue
              no fun,
mommy knows I've become a man
when I sent a list of demands
why she never told me I was Jesus's son and if he loved
to drink before playing with guns yes yes yes go play with your
guns shoot another target your eyes are rabid potent to
get lost in if we want to,
Babylon is make-believe
what I told you make-believe
it's okay you're allowed to leave
to the chanting we plant my seed
growing up now be a good boy
daddy's guns now be a good boy
shooting up now be a good boy
shooting up now to the sun
shooting up now to the sun
Babylon is in the sun
Babylon floods in the sun
Don't wanna hurt lather up with mud and repeat dreams stained
with we cement from construct site plunged into fervor of
motion, don't stop we onna deadline, you fill us in on what
we missing, dead mouse in underpass, feathers dropped by
pigeons nesting but a song stuck in my arm flowing to my head, be
careful you'll feel my pain, oh be careful mother gave my name, hard
to say hard to be more than body limits drop decay, in the piss
sleep away rain water soaking feet no matter mother gave my name,
              and if you want
                we can be the same
              and if you cry

   we can be the same
and if you love
   we can be the same
and if you wake alone
   we can be the same
and if you dream
   we can be the same
and if you die
   we will be the same
you know when we die
   we will be the same
shooting up now
     to Babylon.

Age Appropriate

Sit studious piano keys.
Shatter teeth soft genetic enamel.
Father's dad at fault.
Had the wrong mother.
Soaked dentures in waterfull cup.
How wonderfull, disbelieve time, nope.
Hand-me-downs; blood shared, blood remembers.
Birthdays are no good no more.
Spat out candle flame, celebrate. YAY!
Everyone who left never showed up anyway.
Go figure.
Did not figure it mattered.
Inertia of ideas, aging proportionate to cyclical bucking.
Next ride is better anyway.
Promise

Giver of Curse

Alright,
 we began on a rainy day
 slugging homeruns.
Each thunder ferocious gall
 exploding along hardwood forests chewed by man.
Silvery whisps of age exemplified by voice
 lacking tenacity and proof.
Alright,
 we ended on separate days,
 one before the other messing up calendar.
  Romantic thrown out blood.
  Kings grew out hair and sheared robes to shreds.
  Roosters cawing rebirth of sun peeking up over
                east horizon absolute.
  Understood wedge of dynamos locked together.
        Color wheel reaching beyond space.
    Spatial dimensions aggrandized and feeble.
   Croaking billowing bullfrog throat
       pressing on surface tension pondwater.
  Elastic atomic rebellion warring against interconnectivity.
   Cause of tectonic shift and the product of space-time.
    Re-enacted macro-scale within each fold of brain tissue.
  Cells animalistic in reliance of nest.
      Crack open egg find anatomy of golden spiral.
Pass rites of spring emancipated from winter ice.
Place within place but outside of forces shifting negative to positive.
In atomic code we count the X's and the Oh's.
Belly and lungs expanding to displace position of clouds sinking.
Gravity whimpers in young universe looking to fuck.
Be inside and leave comet trails.
Bulge in warm womb kicking against you can feel it,

the conflict of confines and bubbles and
perceptions suffocating under inky bleak blackness
overwhelming sensual receptors.
Dastardly innovative in the juxtaposition of bodily beings
committed to puncture limits physical and otherwise.

Push, push through to new-consciousness.
Free your
        self from you.

Snake Bathe for Fresh Light

Carried stain into death relay generational.
Sunday morning after rain on blue walk bridge
　snake bathe for fresh light,
　the serpent was blessed by woman.

Bells gong slumber religious visions
of castrated god naked demanding of his beasts,
　　all for the fragile sanctity of polluted idea of control
　　over civility supposedly utopian culture.
Boarded windows,
　rust wire,
　bolted doors,
　　lost city less full and feelin' it, man.

Corruption sunk chemical intake that's better.
　So specific, loosen up, take a different approach.
Limited metaphysical by television by words by color,
　however physical barriers leapt with gusto.

And us monkeys learned how to shave.

Molt

I have lived here before.

Lizard shed husk left, frizzled desert sun we march
 across sands, highlight erratic pinpoints marked by
 pink cactus flowers (luscious pink on drenched green prickly).

Reptilian husk, dried out eyes mouth crackle flakey blood is dust.
Now we stall, examine what evolved from.

Reconceptualize the meaning of resistance.
Ill-advised words raising temperature,
 salt flats out where we renewed mushy beings
 but fall drought stricken thirst,
 bones preoccupied with time,
 vultures winged circle above soon-carcass mummification
 crested gilded indigo patterns of old to be
 swept and buried by forget.
But luck!
The sky swells with massive clouds.
Dynamic bombinations deluge,
 and on burial process a pool of water emerges,
 no mirage.
Shrubs and flies gather as clouds dissipate oblivion
 and crisp light shaft slewn from desert sun on oasis
 born to provide vitality for lost and tumultuous seekers
 passionate enough to believe.

Wide

Wake up with the breath of dawn.
Big world how wide you are.
Grounded, rooted in light,
 slumber in your peace.

And here we are with nothing to fear,
 opened up to everything.
Spectral future shadowing us
 while playing with the sun.

Parker Pickett

House Plant on Window Sill

Window open warm day thank you.
My leaves twist, tussled by breeze.
I motionless in studious gaze about life steady
   and the sun bears an X,
     the mark to reach for.

Oh! Leak through puffy clouds, gallant atmosphere!
     Leak your light to me I desire!
Each gilded shaft a path to rediscover,
           a nutrient to stave off hunger.
    Bathing all the day in warm deluge,
    brimming verdant within small-self.

Lo! How small compared to your immensity!
   A gift for all us microcosms
  sprouted from stems diverging from
   singular trunk, a story of evolution.

Even as I sit silent secret still and solitude surround
       I evolve,
       I never stop.

A fly adrift buzzes rainbow-sheen wing,
  plants feet to leaf I extend,
humbled to receive all such light
   you decide to give.

Cell Walls

It easy.
Light of renewed sun
wiggle particle wave through
fresh budding sharp pure green leaflets.
Light outlining cell walls veins stretching
to breathe for the very first time.
Point digging atmosphere bring
sharp pure green color with, extend life.
Grouped on branch jagged exquisite mess collecting
and being
in obscure forest absent of man's fate.

You Don't Play?

                         In the meantime on a warm day out with
             good vibrations developing madness theoretical ya dig?
Theoretic messages being formulative of young one's conscious being.
   Redbluelights swarming on other side of road busy
       peek eyes the neighbor hood watches and
ponders about another day when maybe there
       wouldn't be such distress.
Blue lines barricading to keep out poor destitute ethnic diverse.
My hands wring out trouble,
 sweating now first of all year.
Dry season is upon us and we gotta get our quench
   with guitar squealing corridor of time.
SMACKing keys lips pursed puffing kiss I refuse yah language abuse.
Not the best but at least does some good
           and that is what it takes.
    Marigold walls cut-throat shade denying glow,
       attainable eyesight not quite all-right.
Plight of yesteryears coming back when speak loud and prosper.
           Televise it in our palms.
            Quote it in our games.
         Signal to ghosts portrayed by mind imaginative.
"hello"
–the world is a drag by the hands of time
 "you don't play"?"
–hows about you and me tumble on with tumbleweeds move right on out
           beyond good moments free ringing joyful
               kaleidoscopic trances melding hues more bountiful than
           home grown gardens dotting pleasant hill leaning with
            sage-green slopes into frothy malicious fury of salt spray shore?
hows about you and me return frazzled by American enterprise and
   our teeth falling out licking rust off our fingers
       ostensibly in pursuit of glory-flory-allelujah

A Fist Full of Flowers in the Big Parade

                and ALL that jazz?
"You sound so forced.
  Tirades of judgement non-requited,
      selected works ye mighty and despair.
          Never felt lower than at night woofing populace steps over
              neglect body concrete back ruminate on incredulous whims.
          To suck smog expel chit-chatter ugly unambitious.
            Consider proud? Helacious idioms vagrant apostles removed
                far from spoken human liberation,
              pocked and corroded morals,
        withdrawn empathy into roughed up pockets.
     Pull out lighter flick pull-drag ashes story of rebellions,
        quick tap and slow burn until gone and tossed on sidewalk
     in busy work of modern man's now-consciousness. How different think?"
–I think the same as all through time.
  At least I am foolish enough to admit it.

History Compression

Gravity hangs with me.
I am property, I matter.
Influence each coping mechanism function
 reacting heart-stop pump again full of fear
 and world watches stumble into own earth, implosion.
From within, destruct from within.

My country tis of thee,
 sweet land of supremacy,
 new fascist regime,
 of thee I bleed.

I don't believe in bandages.
Duct tape never fixed a broken heart.

We touch hands, we kiss.

I lived.
Not long,
but I lived.

Hippiez

All the kids wanna cut their hair,
 get out the world and get jobs,
  own a dog and own some kids of their own.
Function of denial I sit in stupid dumb idiocy
 bawling baby hungry for life.
How we say what we are searching for?
Obtain cane,
 spectacles too,
  walk alone no lover no partner.
Meadow in distance a few yards to sit and tumble mind around lake
 reflection, soldier on excommunicating own tongue from
 values of learned peoples and customs.
An outsider looking in at all the mysteries.
X-pity poem of the selves marked with melodrama.
And the poor getting duped by the rich again and again.
Megachurches with golden crested domes for ceremonial selfishness.
And the poor getting duped by the rich again and again.
Filtering at top of lower classes keeping the lid on tight,
 no allow bubble over.
And those who lucky get release into atmosphere while rest drown boil.
All the kids wanna cut their hair,
 get out of youth and get jobs,
        and vote Republican
        and hoard moniez
        and mutilate empathetic heart for gods of greed
                that demand everything from you;
                for them to control you
                and profit off of your obedience.
All the kids wanna obey
 for discounted nice pay
  to consume things they are told they need to own.

To Another Time

Scratch n' sniff rock n' roll.
Paint peel cinder block wall.
Directionless recruits dive headfirst.
                    No diving, shallow.
Conform to obey.
Obey to be beaten into shape,
                    who's a good boy?
Ears putrid agony plastic siren wail.
Rush to become savior.
Hallucinatory jangling emitted by heat on roads.
                    To another time, I guess.
Spill and shatter crystal ball globe.
Excess turns regress is death too you should know.
   All explicit with rage,
   functioning on no sleep,
   tunes pumping fever radical
   designer tones eclipsing chic standards,
                              aesthetic standards.
No reply
   and happiness ain't too far behind.

Death Knows Death and I Know Death

    Pugnacious now indifferent.
     I am weary.
   Soak in bathwater, drain it.
   Eat sunlight quite hungry.
  Dreams awake me into truth.
 Satin soft hands parting shadows tugging into place wisdom.
How the roads are empty and the wind needs sound to carry adrift
 into eardrums.
Hiding moody vacant mourn bleed a little.
Crush utmost yammering divinity hammering.
Decapitated god he was too loud annoying and possessive.

    And now I realized why we crumble so easy.
    All we thought we knew was built on lies.
    Buoyant above our filth and decay is nothing.
    Images constructed to keep us squirming to top.
    There is nothing up there but vapid stale fraudulency.

Born a poor boy born a dead town born smiles all the same.
Death knows death and I know death.
I know those who not know life I know the value of life.
Where we are free I find and remain humble to be.
Step away from the bottomz and the peakz I demand another way.
Found sea-shells by the seashore and listened to both songs of the sea.
Bloated I puked fear and cleansed coital stupor amore she want too.
Child me would be proud to be alive, just to be alive was nice.
Child me would've touched curiosity naked desirous song and dance.
Expand vibrancy of cities losing culture out in wild America.
Wild America partitioned and relegated to mythos of yore.
Brushes teeth violent her gums bleed spit out toothpaste streaked mirror.
Atomic code unlocks your body all wallz crumble we wash ferocious goop.
Cows of Kansas look up munch herbivores docile behind fenced landscape.

Parker Pickett

Nothing ever mattered much until I remembered
   blue skies cushioning our emancipated design.
      It was an accident,
     our wayward creation.
   Sorting through the consequences of love,
      learning which way to grow.

Decade Dance

Final poem of the decade,
decade dancing under gunfire hellfire
rising peril nose itch.
And beauty in youth lose attraction
as the whole world
revolves and warms
and we pass through changing voices
spreading legs open
to arrive anew,
              or so hoped,
              or so believed.

Swallow Americana

Hey baby,
        I am your factory abandoned
        overgrown with moss and woods.
      Remember when you worked
    in me pump energy between
      my walls my cells?
   Grandfathers labored their factory smoke
plume bring home unsatisfied then
    ride to local bars displaced misery.
         Why did they leave us?
Oh yes,
       dedicated to decay swallow Americana.
        Working class extinct. Put away
      your Jesus, words and lies from him.
     Nothing coming back, all left us mired,
      poverty used and chewed up by machine,
       spat on ground they left us groveling.

        But this bottle,
        it won't leave.

        I won't let it.

Two Thatched Cottages

Billowing psychedelic rust-red to orange pollen gold
curving bubbled by elastic gum grain swollen
in olive green shading, infrared carving out fluid intercourse
    of structure wiggling fierce.
Two puddles meek yet soft blue sky hue liquid membrane
    separate from burnt up heat of evening gradient low.
Faces of houses tinted toasted adobe brick and
      rooftop gritted sullen cyan succumbing to
        afterglow in present state.
My my,
 humble shoulders wide from fieldwork,
 plowing fat of mind, eyes plant images
 sprout to harvest when ready.

Rain Song

i never took you for a morning, you never looked so bad.
 i always knew the only way to start was when you left me alone.
intolerance and choking on the past has left a good mark on tight skin.
if i could dance as well as you would think, borders climbed with pivot
                                                and shake,
                                                rattle,
        onslaught of sleep deprived madness,   and roll.
  not the only one to dine in on words spat fuming heat.
pick up the beat, learning notes,
               detrimental dehumanization preventing
            near pearl shined smile with camouflaged intentions.

  do u c wht i c ?
               caught within a painting on a wall?
lines buried structure fuck your future and this one is holy too.
        all beautiful
        all desire incomplete.
                i am frayed and not the same as you would want.
      when they spoke with big mouth i fought to listen
             such a drag, maaaaaaan.
it is a toad
  relaxing warted under
 soft gray clouds fixing
our dried tongues with rain.

Sketch Under Railway Bridge Next to Wapahani River

   Clouds of swarming gnats riverside mudbank imprint below
     porous beams steel rail bridge set rusting decay of Papaw above.
   Dreamers tagging coloring emotions exotic into neutral backdrop
     earthen glow.
  River flex brown murk of sediment a retroactive passenger shoot up
     rooted hymnal.
Loss of sun with perfect clouds billow as big as they can be and still not
 impeding the growth of others in grand expanse,
reflect mirror shine smooth clay slope fluid erosion.
Path verdant express fresh lung expand inhale,
   eating light in an effort to remain,
 seeds looping fruited armor plump.

Balance of life on display in motion keep quiet or you'll miss each moment.

Territorial claiming remnants of purity foolish,
 retrace millennia footsteps guide simple truth of all.

Rites

    Pulled the seam
     tying us together.

    Articulate in hibernate,
      insubordinate,
    rolled up our cities into sleep.

Practiced serendipitous values
     until found out death was real,
    one of the only real things out there.
 Pardon the tone of being brash and unaware.

       Equate this to luxury and wish for less.
      Shouldering the passion of make-believe
      armed with a yearning to grow as old as the stars.
Ate dust for breakfast nibbling on bones cleaned by microorganisms.
Delicate white poking out of umber fermenting earthen mud.
    Never too old to cry we choose when we want to cleanse.
   Separated bodies from clothes and submitted to primacy,
        revolution in own organs revolting against creation.
    Passage of legislation and time yet we feel safe escaping.
But out crawled song
 and we grew legs in our need to dance.
   Knowledge gained and supplemented by love,
      dug six feet and buried all things above.
    Waiting for the world to bloom flowering
     then pluck each petal, a masterpiece
              torn limb from limb.

There is no return,
    so we move on.

Feathers

There is room.

                    Fish mouth open gulp current.
            Plentiful, talon tore scales placid body.
                    Fish mouth open gulp oxygen.

There is room.

        I bend space filtered by voice,
      conceptualize body admire nothingness
    and if we are absent here,
      we are absent there?

Exist in vacuum of your wooly bleating heart,
herded by love expressions   _____
tended by words calling   / Fencelines are chosen \
and gathering on the | perimeter of where and |
hills rolling green   / how we decide to exist; \
grasses munched peace.   \ We are our own shepherd, |
                                      | our own flock. /
                                      _____/

Happy

       Lifted on a sunny day.
     Braided hair twined with wildflowers.
    Napping city Anderson yawning afternoon empty of traffic.
 Never knew what this is about.
 Never knew when roads would drift to this.
       Understatement on why we're all alive.
Cushion droplets gathering clouds.
          Pollen scent attracting we to we.
Heavy heart buoyed by simple words.
   Two birds pecking trash lined up alleyway.
       Everyone had to give a little more.
    Future full and radiant allure.
   Sifting through plastic,
     mentioned dread wrapping insipid.
   Imagine boundaries.
  No see, know protection.
 Fingernails scrunch black health of earth.
 Spread palms smile as pure dirt crumbles back into soil
 below body toiling away at eternity.

Tag

Two kids play tag
in busy rust town street.

They know
no boundaries.

Now Heaven

Stasis of light
cup sunken eyes,
lift thy lost sight.
Give gracious beat,
roads escape rest,
and no heaven
but this now heaven,
 lifted— —being

Part of that Big Squeeze

Guided by unfavorable starts in voyage of sweltering night.
Pathway endless until abrupt edge of West,
                 of darling songs radio played.
 We met in juicy communion,
  ripe with souls sharing individualistic glory
 defiant and sappy with interludes connecting
       dear life to lurid death.
Abandoned memories kicking bountiful laughter
 along sparkling streets before emergence of dawn,
 before thoughts harvest each plump star shimmering,
 expanding jungled dynamos above our fruited plains.
Spat seeds into earthen lust to foment blessed compassion
 on the way we choose to die,
 folding arms body rest on sidewalk weary as
 playful rats skip between coital dependency and overwhelming
   fear of masses crawling out of gutters to stake their rightful
 claim to bombed out streets tonight.
 Tagged buildings spreading rust into flatlands.
If you could dream as far as Denver
 residing in spine of American, bad luck and when she moans,
                             she moans,
 hollering obscenities to shatter idyllic attributes unfairly painted
 onto her image by minds creating personas that
 want what she will not give.
                      A fine tune buried by chatter
                         yet recovered by action, hand in hand
                  whistling goofy remarks about freckles chain linked
           to so-called regrets, massive uplift of wind curling click
       ribbed roof of mouth.
                           Outside Be Here Now in Muncie
                           a male figure asking for a dollar.
                      He appreciates a whole bunch the gift.

I am repeating actions,
I am giving in.
                        Eat he sez but I don't see no food.
                            Different hunger.
I get it, his smile shuffle off destiny chosen now deliver sincere.

And if you burn, don't burn out.
Ignite in others keep fanning your flames.

"We all part of that big squeeze, you know."
        She chided, she sang.
    I folded with her hips,
       provided temporary bliss but all was gone.
Found me feeding crazed zinging celebratory jaunts
 towards their unbelievable god.
I sit back and watch new ritual performance,
  married by asphalt misgivings rippling esophagus
                      send sound waves
                            shot spacious sky.
 She is the door.
Awakened, croaking,
  open to regain perspective.
                Widen.
"Come through,"
  sez she,
"this will not hurt."

                And so the story
                 goes to bend this
                hour shapeshifting
                atomic codes of a
                bashful sorta love,
                  or something
                      like that.

All My Friends are Deindustrialized

>There is no reason to scream anymore
>now that people won't listen or join in the chorus.

Oh good natured despair coming knocking hello.
Splash in the liquid fire spilt by sundown.
    Papers and words left alone undoing time from our eardrums
    halting progress velocity what no gulp
        the liquid fire spilt by sundown.
Ravaging what world we live in and its values reconfigured,
        letters stained on walls writ with ash.
    Blew it all the way to outskirts Milky Way.
Cut core of tree count rings and age says nothing,
    all about if ready but we are never quite ready all lies
    in minute puerile joust with enamored vitality.

Something about boundaries?
>No trespass
> ah-
>   against us
>no pass us
>dried up and died
>for your wealth.

Me and my friends have been deindustrialized.
Castles made of sand melts into the seas.
Chain-linked hearts, rusted over eyes.
Went as far as death and they still kept wanting more.

Hard Water

Hang over head social construct.
I am poor and I know it.
Pulverized by loss, by diseased afflicted
                              en masse.
No escape let's lose our minds and dance anyway.

Hard water pour down throat for painful thirst.
Steel has a flavor of its own.

      "This ain't suffering, just unpleasant. Work harder."
What I'm told by fucks who don't know
    the pangs of starvation or
    the rot of imperfect teeth.

Oooooh,
    let's bless an angel,
                          cheers.

Beards

Candle filled by flame wax and she texted me saying to come on out
she wanted the fuck and I say no too busy meandering on paper and
not between such vapid erosion with you spread to dive in and conquer.

I underline my faults depleted of brutality and of cops beating
us senseless because they have the badge and the supposed
authority every slip is a slide not to get it wrong,
when scared and people sit at Brass Ring pounding drinks to
    enlarge chances of escape and
drowning owe you the hearsay oh jolly two guys go out back
and slip the slide of tongues pants off cocks sparring and they tease
each other,
bearded tease of fun and horny and how is this bar closed now the faces
 coast on homeward fortunate to find if luck be a lady.
The surface broken.
I hang up.
Itch my back.
Close eyelids and transport lungs forward
to not be moving,
to not be coming back.

                  Menace of humanity writ in haste
                     to denounce public trust.
               I am one who is too far to want to love
               or confide silly overrated secrets with
                     masters of dreams and of realities,
                 movers and shapers of all.
       So shut the door, honey,
         shut the door, man,
           let's leave this place and be done with tonight.

Classic Buzzkill

                Unbelievable.
Oh almighty fangs puncturing breastplate seeping venoms.
   Color of bloods transfigured and fizzing noxious fumes,
      getting ready to dizzolve cellular walls of cardiovascular system.
     Burn down all systems and replace with sound.

FRRRRRRRRRRRRRRRRRRRRRRRRRRRRRRRRRRRRRREEDOM

              Man it is the collapse of ROCK 'N' ROLL.
            Who cares for the radio you classic buzzkill?
          Cleaned out ears in demand for something new.
         Behemoths risin out of snapped tone,
    crackling kindred erroneous chords mangled along new frontiers,
      eroding along already plundered routes of escape,
   silk road tattered and rip, stain, trampled into history.
Meals eaten and forgot because we have touched and we have lost.
Kind but negligent.
It is a poem if I say it is a poem.
It is the same old song and dance herding gullible masses into
    fucking frenzy,
 bawling peeling own flesh to get after I feel and remain hidden
    on sidewalks
 drumming eulogies something better masticating gibberish.
You growl for and earfull well here is enough for both ears.
              Gargling the drag.
              Venture into pleasures.
            Hip ugly rodeo big tenting down blvd.
                I am surprised
              (only after I pretend)
                 on occasion
            (get away with it).

Pocket Globe

Stick hand into sun grasp light.
No burn, no burn, cool as water,
backs breaking in the fields.
 (this land is your land, too)
What would we leave behind?

There is a globe in my pocket.

What is the sun to the globe in
                my pocket?

Political Fervor

               Ad infinitum;
        the sun helps me cope.
          My labor unwinding,
              your voices switch emotive patterns,
            birds glitch and warped warbles denounce victory.
      Pleading for future on no not again.
    Acquired reason to assume negligence is afoot.
      Cause of travesty global wreck,
        coffee is defunct,
        cocaine too plain overrated,
        been slapped awake too many times from personal coma
                no wake up no more.
Squeeze atoms from rainbows
   mixing together the folly of racial divide,
           our hands congealing from displacement
              and now we have solution!
         Until brutality vaults those penetrating wails,
            lingering scent of ignition and blood.
          Spectacle of disaster create disturbance.
      We masses commune and praise dead rightfully so.
    Crossbones reinforced by loose-toothed skull
and I, meager white stupidity unbecoming,
          birth songs from the ether of emptiness.
          Raging vindictive nebulous indictment
            simplifying closure and sadness for the common human
                  grasping quiet despair.
              Hair drifting as we ride each other and
                limit values embarking and ostracized from land
              waking trance metabolic resurgency eclipsing all
            known moons cratered in your expansive eyes.
      Brick bashing skull of invertebrate parasitic siphoning it is
        the unification of our fragile hearts that allows

me to be transparent as well as elusive,
        yawping isolation remember liberation
imprinted into our gratuitous beget?

                Stomped and trampled by political fervor;
                     and the bodies will weep
                       uncoagulated rivers of
                        sadness washing all
                          function of death
                            back into the
                                sea.

Generational Blue

Let him hang there
    he ain't no thang.

                (pause)

Image in head
also reality.

                (pause)

Stuck on you
and everything you do.

                (pause)

Hey mr. officer come
beat to a dried pulp.

                (pause)

Apparently asked for it
so says their fuck-law and dis-order;
dying from your greed.

                (pause)

To flex against
then be tried and ruined
 by wicked odious machinations
   of American police brutality.

Oh Progress, I Love You

      To be sent for among our dainty city
      rocking out with ugly rhythms
      cranking out jams to groove during so-called
          apocalypse.
      Big men have trouble hiding.
      Big men roll up their dicks.
      Big men wetted dreams and suckle for mommy.
      Big men bite hard not let go tongue tip circling
          lathering with spittle
          trickles of blood
          it ain't right that we
          break our bonds too early.
      Big men wanna lie so theys can uh… get hands up in explore,
          not quite rude just unpleasant and sad.
Bad, bad hands, you do so much wrong you bad, bad hands I punish.
Big men;
bad, bad hands.
   Big men extinct, down with the dinos,
        scales feathers and all knocked aside by history
           and progress.

Oh progress, I love you,
   you sweet gentle troubadour parade significant eulogy by way of
     limber mouth whipping out words that seem
    to linger far longer than any sort of dysfunction
     caused by obstructionists high up in the ranks of our
      floundering politics.
 I told you about those ugly rhythms?
 But I wanna dance ugly too, I wanna scream all to hell and a
   ham-basket-head,
    wicked, masticating ridiculous claims of fortune even if we bold
     as can be, this time no favor.

Parker Pickett

Put head
on rounded knee.
There there.
We walk amongst our former and future selves
       praying to gods that never have and
               never will exist.

To Death Where We Part

        When we left the stars
        and settled for a 9 to 5,
    weekend carousing with the pals
        slamming feet around town
          pausing under streetlights
            moths gathering around light
                bashing head into light.
          Lunatics of the streets rocking back on haunches
           and howling mad-gabbing towards the moonlit sky.
"Ahhh forget it, man,
    let's go home,
  I'm tired of tonight."
              It never made sense.
            Train in distance Indiana swooning,
          comfort of easy livin, more or less.

        She once made galaxies swirl
        and shook stardust from her hair
        and had many men revolve around her they did merciless
            those cratered moons begging for
            her gravity imbued by love.

A forest trembles
in gust of wind.
As cities die
we still pretend.
Who contains who
our borders defend.
Once there was song
not wrong to rescind.
            Fascination with stars while
            digging down into hardened earth,

                from fish
                    to monkey-/-from monkey
                            to man-/-from man
                                      to death where we
                                            part.
      I've drawn constellations in her eyes.
        I've sent rockets to her moon.
        I've observed her meteoric descent from dynamos
            onto lilliputian world,
                a world not quite big enough to
                satisfy her magnetic desires.
If our flesh could achieve
greater balance, pausing under streetlights,
body hunched along brick wall delirious
                    rising from primordial slobber.
            Now so, so far away from
                her expansive heavens
                      astounded by above.

Perishable Delight

Perishable delight of big small town
and he don't want to lose again
but he no stop
    he do and do and do and not for own health.

Each passing day we resemble characters
    in stories of old,
    extend genetic codes each page added.
Continuity, immortality.
Squandering atypical ascension through
practice of grooming to replace
when societal roles have been fulfilled.

I hope he defies conventions,
    the beauty of free-will.

Redevelop Communion

Supply demand needs oh feeds,
it ain't an illusion scent
 of melted butter on lips cooked food now full.

She moaning tabletop.
 Pouncing for bite
       delectable,
 I push face overboard.

In service of the self.
I remainder of us.
 We redevelop communion.

        What do we call it?
            Bliss?

In Defiance of Death

   Struggle of learning lessons and retaining information
when wanna open window explore woods divide property
illusion of lines, of color on pages by sheepish so-called prodigies,
swallow lump in throat, ain't too scared of monsters reviled,
gutter-mouthed scooping with teeth forked claws the filth
swept by acidic rainfall onto oily city streets fierce and
              dangerous in image.
            Create to destroy.
Fine tuned elliptical surge momentum.
Hang from doorways monkey children.
   Future not believed but here we are,
   swollen with breasts open and cock received an appetite
   calmed by desire and suction, hormonal functioned click,
   a possible thought of emotion and therefore it is cliché
     baby,
  that I be alone in my life
 and you be alone in yours but here we are now and then.
Whistling blues all hail death is closure forced reconcile utter doom.
Perilous jump heart to tantrum beat collide sick disease as one can be.
Social advocacy of drugs and their respective release.
Climb walls get out pit of despair.
  It's these surroundings, man,
  and this selfish outlook snared feet worn, shake chains in motion,
  succumb to supple touch under halcyon sunfade.
 Woke up bathed neon light surprise find dear friend distance.
More than years, time no real.
Hostage contemplate tempt rival euphoric sense of justice
pound meaty fists, knuckles jagged dynamos above puncture
                  eyes puncture skin,
           'member first dance rainfall?
Spread mud body undressed, found ritual natural intent to explore,
                         to act.

Parker Pickett

Plume smoke frolic merry saturate memory repeat in liquid surface tense
dissolve spread now mud body quest of youth,
      Animalia we surrender to,
  domain instinct purposeful revive.
Swung futures by rivers cleanse radiate elegant mannerisms,
         you sorry lot,
conflict designed games protracted carve triangles form absorb
  resolve and no,
      not this one.
These results are pitied and no reward!
Center emptiness vanish returns until send out for no returns!
In conversations leaning to speak close barbarism in bar static noise,
    there ain't no truth here.
A pattern devised played out circles forever, not the answer so what?
Giggle incompletion, prayer for lack of curiosity which does kill the soul.
        LACK OF CURIOSITY KILLS THE SOUL.
Fouled by useless gimmicks bent by polluted receptors of senses,
unable to digest and make much sense of anything.
   What a conundrum!
Social enemy positioning for dominance, male to female to all pursuing
       to define so as to reason with existence.
A mockery what a mockery shadowed by absolute disgust on way we walk,
      heel toe heel toe.
And difficult to recover from blunder of affectionate fools such as I.
     It ain't over, we ain't older yet.
Maybe last a few days, don't have much to live anyway so why not live
         to one day die?
Surrender to fate as did Achilles in battle Achaean beauty rage outskirts
      fabled walls hilltop honey mythos Troy.
Surrender to fate as did John Henry gasp final breath protectorate of natural
  power defender from gaping mechanical maw of industrial perversion.
And in you passionate divinity clear skies look up to airplane sonic
  waves ozone,
  bounce off celestial navigation claiming madness in theoretic night.
  Bout time the tongue went babel.
Yawping dimensional yet unwavering we are the same and incomplete.
Powerful delusional curse of free-will and of make-believe.
Provincial heartache only felt when skimming on your surface.

A Fist Full of Flowers in the Big Parade

      Accidental sway to oriental rising,
        occidental overtones blasting from
          conical speakers shivering particles
      out past capability our ears of tin.
Fruited display lapping at feet the damned ruination
bubbling out past breakers and tide pools and self-imposed rules,
combing through fields speckled by farmers and meth addicts
    and business profile and blue suede shoes scuffed music from
   joy of dancing the great dance. Whether alone or together it don't matter
we all end up alone. Took me a long time to realize that.
Circling spaces of birth and death, cupping child eyes in retrospection
    of freedom.
You are beautiful burning edges of loose paper caught forgot
  corner building
    sidewalk smearing ink, small in giant purposeless metropolis.
 My pale skin in disbelief,
     this ain't quite exact,
     an explanation an adventure.
Small epiphany with quick trigger finger gun goes off firing above five shots
RAT…RAT-RAT-RAT………RAT! car following leaving that's right,
                           be afraid as I am afraid!
Protection in damnation of trials and tribulations descending down
 one-way streets elevated by barriers of wreckage and our
colossal blunders overlooked by sanctioning those who are not celebrated!
        Those who eat shit!
        Those who die in euphoric starvation!
Welding frameworks of rust flowers bloom behind wire fences,
  I am your factories forgotten and now decorated by bravery
    and honesty and silence.
                        (pink and blue, I love you)
Planned a garden in you I'll water it every now and then.
 Lots abandoned just doing what was taught what was learned.
Fury evolved and now what? I filled with shame forgive my own,
                I yearn to be held soft and loved with
                  maternal voice calm bashful thick skill,
             no complications of such dreary worlds collapsing
          outdated everywhere we seem to be.
I don't believe in any god nor do I care to.

I only believe in this defiance of death,
   playing along, loving madly, the good fools that we are.
     Mewling babies birthed between floodplains of majestic Babylon,
     spread out both rivers revitalize, carry thirst and language in flow.
   When world widened uncovered we thought too much and gluttonous.
Brain cells with opium padded, eat the lotus.
Smooth transition when release ego and superstitions as hand lifts
dandelions puff blowing, kissing to taste each other
in zenith euphoric bestial stupor. Earth covered, step into dancing
invertebrae fear then relax. Accept. Molecular return to animal,
to primal belly drumming ritual before fabled Eden, before constricting
western civilized idea controls future rampant.
One escapes in eulogized petrichor Mesozoic.
 The mud foment bloom the pollen, the nectar juices of Animalia.
 Man self-proclaimed king of Animalia,
  so far removed from kingdom and
    subjects and birth and
     first breath. Remember,
    surrender, give back into instincts.
Return to the state of primordial mud-bank crawl from water,
    lungs siphon oxygen from air and the world was
  free and
 open and
real.

Subtitled Politic

I've resolved nothing.
I've evolved enough to understand.
Being appreciates being, is and is not is.
Belly America beast prepared jealousy intent.
Sirens bag bodies lock up financial lucrative.
People need something to do.
Self-sabotage is something to do, so do.
Treason class war television hallucinate.
Never too crazy, to think.
Gas demands and forces tear ducts to wetted.
Death demands occupy streets tight fists unwavered.
We scream for each shot for each murder.
Add them to the mountain of American history.
I sent an arrangement of flowers.
I believe smashing the state.
I grieve, I play pretend.
Masks over masks.
Hidden our hide.
A home protectorate all defensive.
Just gonna stay inside and none of this will blow over.

Chivalrous

    Crucifixed hole in heart.
     Let it drip
          drip
              drip all-ways.

    Prudent cleanliness retorting melancholic side-effect,
    I listened to you speak now hear me out, man.

Forged armor we well below the baseline objective,
              fingers coiled around visions of grandeur,
         fleet wind wrestling limbs
        somber willow tree
          sighing through ages who cares?

You've got a coffin waiting for you,
I've got a coffin waiting for me,
 splendid!
              Shall we do the damn thing?

    If ever there was a moment to cry, it was yesterday
               and so we missed our chance.

        Chartreuse canopic covering,
          our organs delayed,
      verdure of earthen domain sprouts.

      What is missing is our
        final words
         set in eroding stone.

Derby

  What do you mean in passing?
Stroke laughter on bridge pillar grafitto pink,
    uprising river swelling humble mouth.
      Is that what is meant?
People motorized roll on over,
    tear down fences,
    burn our cathedrals,
   whisper to each and every in ruins,
                      in sadness.

Atop green hill grass under trees big eternal growth,
   shade of millennia,
  youthful battles hopping and rolling downhill
                  non-motorized,
   blood in games below hoisting trophy prized champions,
                            gone.

Madison Avenue baseball diamonds.
Toppled rust fence chain break grass cover mound of memories.

  Age settles quick upon these bones.
  No floodplain glory no more.
     Ease under sunfade western,
        as does always.

In Relation to Belated Pleasure

You open up too far off dimensional void.
Shut door can't hear yah speak too frigid that
cosmic gust'll make you sick check it.
Poisoned violet hues revolting to observe catastrophic
malnourished expose on what might not matter.
Melting in special dog day sun,
>   woofing mutts kicked by village elders both panting
>   rocket for scenic passerbye
get outta them hormones, man.
Chemically bankrupt long afterward voices
diminished in belated pleasure.
Caught them jives on wounded street parading
astronauts vectoring search for
>   paid passage to sector love, physical,
>   to touch hands, a tool,
>   monetary a tool to use, physical.
Exploring to ease sedation social commentary
on communion of raggedly assed no toothed compadres
keeping composed under pressure of exploitation.
"You too political"
>   I hear but you speak sideways,
snickering slint of stupidity slighted with shameful
snap sight shut tight sickening searing separation of
seductive soul and sorrowful sound sent sealed and
sabotaged self unsatisfied in season of setting dog day sun,
supposedly superfluous,
sedentary misgivings secretly scarring somber suggestions,
secondary only to you,
>   *sweet thang.*

After Detonate

Never quite had an approach other than this one.
Brevity of direct yolling everyman exasperated and declining by way
of modern America crumble by crumble radioactive decay.
America was also wounded by the
dropping of both bombs.
Atomic radiation in our thoughts,
we delivered the blow and are haunted by
vile acts put on another. Trauma begets trauma.
Large hammer has made dent in skulls,
blued bruised coagulate ideas to harden and sharped into stone.
Arrowheads piercing any sort
of deliberate defensive wall around
loss of heart and de-wilding our natures,
synced into world tight neck
superrobotics all about the economo, baby.
I've grimaced in diluted rage from
whiplashed decisions embarked with nuanced agony,
supple trends in marketplace of our total collective
and those who are ridiculed on the ragtimes.
Hey yousa vacuum of empty space.
No stars no dust filtered,
no examine through microscope no
lens to enlarge the distance,
no amorphous bodies of matter shift
and shape our dimensions abroad.
How such tough hands plush when catapulted into
bigger bodies of dense materials and bones squish with
sickened sigh and capitulated organs say they have had a day,
by golly.
Lapped up all I can chew get on with it,
sorry blemished foolish baritonal speak barbed tension,
all the goddamn dreary day, all the goddamn life,
all the won-ton viciousness, if sadness would suffice.

Break the Cycle

Juniper trees I blow their bloom across ocean,
hollow clouds excavated for golden shafts of light
chucked out from heavens to earthen lust,
raising exotic monuments for prophetic voyages.
Bold and disastrous why they even attempt.
Seduction of animals with hunger.
Found epiphanies glazed on the warble of chickadees.
Neglecting baby yawping in ache of baby-mind expanding
all to return to ferocious goop.
Blended by genetics and spat out of billowing tongue mouth agape.
You have been spoken and therefore been found.
Messy articulation of sunflowers ripe with seeds of fire soaking earth.
Yellow derived from green the first color seen by any eye opened to
the dawn of universe glitzing effortless expanse attainable with song.
Permeating vast rolling fields held together by youth whistle while work.
The taste of peaches hovering bees suckling juices crisp flesh.
Tender wars neglected by all-encompassing starry eyed crossed
    lovers pouncing
on the chance of salvation
marred in orange splendor.
Decorate rusting families memorizing photographs and how each
                  smiled the way we tend to smile.
Undertones of jazz on the static tension
from hallucinatory rebellions existing in mind
and on this page.
Traversing verse and guided by manic clarity,
to define borders is our own elated choice.
Gradual swell realizing and then faltering and smoothing placid glass,
gone,
our bodies give out and we escape into another body
continuing the trend of
gorgeous,
beautiful annihilation.

Cheap Politic

The Empire is dying!
It's official, public betting on collapse.
Bubble filled with hot air,
  breathing the Big Lie.
Heartland bloodrust, rot inside out.
Diseased, spreading.
The coasts can only glisten for so long.
The consume can only devour for so long
  before all that's left to devour is
  own mass, own body.
Body filled with hot air.

History will not be fond of us.
Politic hides erosion well.
A good smile with cheap words goes far.
Well, I'll be a monkey's uncle,
  do we go all in? Take what we can get?
The sacking of Rome.
The pillaging our own.
Haven't we seen this before?

There will be someone who comes forth
  during hysteric collapse.
They will claim to have all answers, to be strong,
  to be a savior of the damned.
They have nothing, they lie.
They want control, they want power usurped.
When they come forth, we say NO.
We defy them. We must defy them.
It is time to let the Great American Beast die.
Only then can we move forward.
Only then can we evolve.

Humane

How tall the shelves of history rise
 and continue this moment gone.
Soft people decompose hard people
 petrified to stone,
 and to stand alone searching for cosmic calling,
  feathered shadow falling
  from reflective heavens into
 swollen eyes of gaiety mesmerized by truth.
Fluxuated between soft and tough skin,
 skin a barrier to believe in
  to break down
  to beyond body.
To touch is an attempt at penetrating physical barriers
 containing human spirit.
Captive and animalistic I place hand upon their shoulder
 recanting reassurance.

Let yours be freedom basking in humane love.

Vicious

                Combing the streets all hours
                   begging hard truths coming round the sharp corners
               enigmatic hey baby you are floundering
          rolling all wiley in profuse sweat coma.
                Veins are pumping and hands are tactile,
            wishing for the best if there was ever such a thing.
     Maybe when gunshot wakes me up I can and do
                      believe in miracles.
Harmless, is what they say
  to moonlight rippling somber across
  spacious bay waters.
                        Made it worse when I was encapsulated by
                        notorious love, good omens for a life
                            lived destitute.

Folding thoughts
tuck into sleep
apparent naked
stark gray of
rainfall dawn
woodpine fence
old natural fence
guiding limits to cows exploring
                    roaming
            in search of holier hills filled with plentiful grass to be
                munched until mud.
We've been expressed a thousand and some odd times
by stumbling derisive dialogue
coating our senses with outward faults
be received and collect
humble felt gregarious blue summoning solace of ocean sized harmony
melting omnipotent laws rectified in our houses disheveled abandoned.

Parker Pickett

I filter voice of mother,
sedated belated now recovered,
how harsh it was to wake and
cleanse a wound that would never quite heal.

Even Cowgirls Get the Blues

   I heard you buried your ache
out back where all the cowgirls
       sing the blues.

   Longing for some sunshine
hugs from mom carried asleep
      saved every old excuse.

     Shovel top pat pat
spade-head cut into earthen
   however far we want to go.

Oh to reclaim peace and poverty
   from anxious hands groveling
      sunk innocence low.

I found some words to share with hope that sudden shock of being alive
would fuel a rise from gravesite erasing epitaphs but alas,
        too late,
        too sweet a gilded death
           adorned by tears infused with song lyrics
          strummed by blistered hands
             too tired to dig anymore.

I Reckon

        Change the channel,
            that emotion hurts too much.
'CLICK'

            It was a radical message
              during radical times.

            Shifted, all things all at once shifted,
              a majestic storm calling for tingling bolts
          shot jag scar through atmosphere,
                the stark empty curling.
              w o w . . . .

          In every dream
              there is a cure.

          Brought to our world decay brilliant.
                  Our hearts first then our hands
          and final our eyes so we can look
              back to reconcile our masterpiece
            splattered raucous strokes
              undulating trail.

Picturesque,
so-to-speak.

              Empty cup on windowsill weeks now spot,
                dug up and buried reactions prepared to drop.
              But the birds sang
                and one could forgive.

        Standing at the door,
           knocking.

Freed From the Bonds

        Your eyes are more tender than you think,
        soft and pressing the room silent wisps
        revealing old memories of childhood playing
            hide and seek in the folds of gray matter,
        what's the matter? Taught too much?
    Break the bonds of birth,
        skip rejoice such pain is gone.

                      Goodbye to guilt.
                      Goodbye to shame.

I am here to sing the thoughts
and love unknown to be known,
passed by language emote.

        Piss in toilet all the kids
        shooting each other in the streets
        ruined by the disadvantages provided
        by the state oh have fun enraged pow teach
    lessons from misguided threats sorry families I am in
    silent remorse but know the unknown and sing the good
      song stick to the best young heart refilled.

Celebrate the achievement.
Wild ecstasy flowing eternal.
Fountain of youth in heart if
found before death.

        My heroes chromatic up down hear them ring
        stroke words all-mighty and be despair,
        hand abundant fruit seeds tugged by tongue
        pressed a few inches into earth to sprout grow.

Hey there,
    you in merriment!
    You beautiful comradery demanding for a chance we all are born with!

I embrace your longing for home inside your self,
    gratitude begotten from magic and effects.

                  To be lost
                 only to return
                and so it is.

Glorious.

A Return to Birth

Pupils wide hazy lights glimmering when eyelids closed in dark of no
light undercover in bed naked and not stoned, breathing OHM and keep
tethered to this world. Put on music nod slow incantations of new birth.
Breakthrough in consciousness, dealing with the shock of it all.
I surrender and spoke uneven, meadows entrenched with flowers help
them spread beyond limited imitations of beauty. Saw me when I was
truly crazy, drooling hysterical naked on kitchen floor a few years back
now, laughing uncontrollable and sudden halt turn dead eyed exclaimed
                "Calm down"
I breathe in new vision.
Sound of eternity wild embalming futures with joy as well as sorrow.
It was the wheel that gave us proof of evolution.
It was the death of your gods that proclaimed man delusional beauty.
Why is my hand weak?
Why is my body loose?
  Atoms dematerialize,
       love fissured apart each slow pump of nutrients leaking
     all over missing the point I think.
        We all talk jargon
          exclusive demeaning talk.
           Grease expunged formalities we caretake for the dead I
       wait all night to release the dead,
          chills overheating.
Simple, and I am scared but it is okay I know it.
              Fruit bearing from coherent divine madness
                expressed devoted for years in quiet
              provisional love with all life
            square shoulders and feet huffing for a new day
        to worship with some words and maybe a smile.

It is all unclenched.
Snap the tension and we are here to follow.

Parker Pickett

I miss my mom and dad.
I miss my brothers.
I miss all my friends.
I miss myself and now it is gone.

Oh Brave Ulysses!

>Oh brave Ulysses eager for home!
>Aimless meanderings always adjacent to love,
>chased off by furious storms no
>mortal could persevere, the gods remain bellicose,
>the sea desolate and time in decay.

Oh brave Ulysses defiant of fate!
Stretching memories thin and bereft of strength,
war taught you well and victory shook your spine fed by the
winds of change.
Warrior cunning magnificent leader valor among men you
stumble Mediterranean folly wreckage disastrous along each
ever more dire shore,
you bleed the same as all life,
you weep ferocious stoic silence harborage of pain.

Oh brave Ulysses!
Death follows your shadow each choice until only you and
you alone walk upon humble earthen land of home,
haunted by cataclysmic war and by fellow men who loved you
and walked through each wrath enduring for you with you
until the struggle capitulated their will and choked
them sunk to the bottom of the sea leaving only you,
heroic wayward seafaring love to return.

Ulysses!
Oh, brave Ulysses!
Hear me call to you across the sea waves!
Hear me cry your name adrift yearning for home!
Ulysses!
You stand valiant along coastline of your Ithaca,
tide slow to rise bubbling froth at your feet,

    silent in remorse for all death left in your
        memories detailing the brutal sojourns of your return!
           Ulysses, I am with you!
                I stand on the shoreline of my love unwavering!
                I wail into the immensity of death oncoming!
                I return resurgent from voyage beyond edge of fate
                                          eternal!

Oh brave Ulysses!
    Shed your fractured heart and be absolved of all ache weary
        bones the blueprint to history,
            and your lonesome ruinous courage
                resolved within the seas of
                    elastic time.

Is this the End?

Is this the end?
 They say flowers will bloom in the end of time.
 They say the kids will go to bed at sundown as the old go out to live free
  and wild, riding on trains of psychedelic dynamite into one last hurrah,
  the final burndown of the final day in the end of time.
 And music will resonate across landscapes and poetry will ignite and burn,
  burn until all language blows one last kiss to reconcile with joyous fate,
  language become drifting ashes caught from the atmosphere with
   our tongues
  so we can say "LOVE" one final time.
 And on the beaches you can see waves turn from our shores, tired of
  the relentless pounding on sweet earth, crests folding into shimmer
  blued horizon, chaos swelling and subsiding into a lucid acceptance
  of attrition for itself, the oceans rest easy in the end of time.
 And all monuments take down their gilded words exhaled by dead men,
  and all statues step down from their marbled thrones, understanding
  that nature has finally run her course.
 Every window will be open, every mouth motionless. Cars will pull to the
  sides of every beat up nowhere road, holding strings attached to balloons
  inflated with wishes and dreams, released by trembling hands with
   looks of forgetful regret slipping out of all peoples,
  stoic facing west, cars humming
   until one by one they die
  and are left parked to rust with the end of time.
 Trees will say nothing more for they know and have seen all, swaying in
  supple rhythms aided by wind, living out this final chapter of time.
 Cities will turn off all lights to remember how the stars look up above in
  the oncoming darkness of the end of time.
 The dynamos will be left to float in primordial consciousness, pull the plug
  the children will drain the tub as they run out into the final day, knowing
  their youth will not be wasted, they will always have a twinkle in their eyes
  for it is the end of time and they will no longer grow older.

There will be no more questions, there never were any answers,
  the religious will cry, the spiritual will sigh, relief will echo through
  each society that lasted to the end.
The truth to humanity will be remembered at last,
  just in time for a smile at the end of time.

That is what they say will happen.
That is what they say will happen in the end.

I,
  in the end,
will be sitting criss-crossed
  in an open field of soft, vibrant green grass,
with the clouds pure and comforting,
  with the sky a euphoric sweet Indian Summer blue sky,
without clothes, naked except for beard and hair,
  with a budding flower in front of me
as I sit there, facing West,
  and the flower tastes life,
and I smile,
  and there is unity,
and I say, "LOVE",
  and there is
no more.

Going Back to Anderson

Never thought that something would occur.
Everyone still talks about the factories.
Only thing left is a smokestack.
It's okay, malls are dying out.
Can we talk about something else?
Don't go to Kroakerheads, too many people I know.
Still are different sides to railroad tracks.
If YMCA basketball taught anything.
If PAL Club football brought anything out of us.
If Little League baseball was still swinging for the stars.
Yeah, we had the magic of the Wigwam.
    We had.
Vacant, looming, hummmmming.
Mosaic, eulogy of romanticized mythos, manifest.
There was a kiss blushing on playground, little zest.
Sweet, sweet kids.
Sweet, sweet opioids.
Being born in death, strangling.
But we swam in the Wapahani anyway.
Emily would paint masterful, express life.
Poems with Hunter downtown alley midnight speakeasy.
Fights at skatepark, drug dealing, cops are Fascists.
Nigel on skateboard, gnarly, good light.
Drill Alaska transcended our decay with sound, holy music.
Legends of the Deep House.
Let's walk to Ricker's.
North Side Middle School closed too?
Sky blue water tower iconic.
Grandparents house now bank parking lot.
That was a good climbing tree.
Zen Garden Shadyside, alone meditate.
Frisch's big boy full of local baby boomers, talking 'bout factories.
Ring the King.

Parker Pickett

The smile tells it's Payton Wells.
Salem, Amber, Dusty and I piano downtown gazebo, rust song.
Sybilla and Josh, Burdock House, refuge music community.
Post-show donuts, deluxe.
Library books overdue, it is fine.
Homeless gather library, refuge rust belt community.
Maybe if there were any opportunities.
Mattress side of street, stained, tired.
Scent in abandoned building, ghosts sighing, family failure.
We wanted sex, parked among cornfields and stars.
We wanted sex, but beat ourselves up at the bars, cheers.
The factories, oh the factories.
What it means to be deindustrialized.
We barely make a difference, those of us still alive.
Yeah, we had the magic of the Wigwam.
    We had.
Pilgrimage to Mounds and pray.
Pilgrimage to Mom's and play.
Streaking at night on golf course under moonlight.
Let our parents drink their misery.
Let us drink their misery, too.
Jump off rooftops into pool, cops called, party over, scatter into cornfields.
Bike ride alone broken pedal pushing escape, daylight, empty
    spring cornfields.
Always nice, to ponder cows, lean on wire fence watch grazing beasts.
Always nice, goofball friends sharing breakfast keep hope alight.
Drum circle solstice pilgrimage to the Mounds and pray.
Ice cream summer cartwheeling grass, sit Fraizer's Dairy Maid.
Poured coffee and spoke of idealistic behavior, hope saved.
Explore our city of nothings and find the somethings hidden, yes.
Climbed fire escapes to top of towers downtown night view, collective awe.
Homeruns we always dreamed of having.
He found a brick from factory rubble pile and took it home.
What was once yours was also once mine.
Hey hey, what it means to be deindustrialized.
All of what we did, all of what we said we could do.
You know,
 if we could go back we would change nothing.

www.ingramcontent.com/pod-product-compliance
Lightning Source LLC
Chambersburg PA
CBHW031315160426
43196CB00007B/542